Journeys

By

SENISTAR ™

Journeys by Senistar
Publisher: God's Water Entertainment
Copyright, 2007 © All rights are reserved. Senistar™
ISBN: 978-0-6151-5481-7

A word from the author:

Thank you for purchasing my first book; Journeys. It features familiar mediums such as poetry that we use to gain higher spirituality and understanding. It gives me great pleasure to share what I believe could help families throughout the world. Too many of us have children and are afraid to speak with them. Too many of us have children and are hesitant when it comes to teaching them. There is an extreme imbalance in the current cultivation of society as it relates to education of our children.

My stories in this book are fictional. However, they are based on some profound truths. In fact these stories are based on actual facts of life, seen and unseen. Most of us can relate to the first story. As for the second and third, well let's just say you will soon be able to relate, all of you! You'll know what I mean by that statement as you witness the signs in the heavens sure to come to your city or town. Some of you may already know what I'm talking about here; the "Mother Ship". Ezekiel saw this great city in the sky in a vision. Do you know this prophet?

These stories are for the young and old, the readers, the skimmers, the believers, and those skeptics. This book is for you to enjoy. Always remember belief in truth will save your life!

Journeys was written with both parents and children in mind. There aren't any pictures in the story portion. I wanted you as parents to create the suspense, and inspire visions with your own spirits for your children. When I started telling stories to my child it was a challenge but I knew that I could do it with the help of Allah (God). So I remembered those who told stories to me in the past like scout masters at scout camps, teachers at school, and some friends and family. They were naturals, story tellers who needed no graphics or gimmicks and by far were the best. In the beginning I stood on those memories, said a prayer and gave all the credit to Allah (God) for inspiring me to give my child a blessed send off into a few hour **journey** better known as "rest".

I remember one day in Chicago during a Saviours' Day Convention; I witnessed a man jump out of his car like a rabbit. He made waves with his arms just to give clear directions. Needless to say, it was easier to get to our destination, and who could forget that? Parents, when reading these stories to your children, be very animated in your presentation. Speak the words as if you are really there. You might want to read it to yourself first so you can get a feel for the stories **before** reading them to your children. Choose a different voice for each character and try your best. This is all our children ever hope for anyway. That we will do all we can to help them explore their minds and souls within this vast world we call earth (Asia).

I hope this inspires parents from all walks of life to be more creative at teaching their children and encourages a greater family unit. I also hope that the truths are taken seriously!

My only regret: I wish I had recorded the stories I told my son for the past several years. Only the Lord knows what was lost, the value, and whether or not it can be replaced.
I believe I make up for that by the end of this book. Enjoy!

Table of Contents

The Mark of Senistar™

This logo represents what appears to be a snake. However, if you look closely it's a bird that eats snakes!!! There is a snake in its beak. The hiding of its wings is as the Son of Man who hides His power (my favorite hero). It is the official trademark of Senistar. When you see it, watch out! Not all hood dwellers are thugs; some are Saviours', and truth warriors.

The Meaning of Senistar™

Senistar means "send a star" or "a star sent" We (the righteous) are Senistar. Don't waste time looking up the words its Latin root, because it was not inspired by anything other than the spirit of Allah (God). It may as well be Arabic.

SENISTAR ™

Official Trademark

Poetic Journeys

SENISTAR ™

Why Cry, I Still Love You?

This was your hands, my pain.
This was your foresight, my pain.
This is you now, my love.
I survived your kiss.
I survived the killer, and the choke of Aids.
You served your purpose, an old soul.
You were the beautiful, they warned.
Nothing left to hold in my arms.
I miss you so much, do you ever cry?
Have you not the knowledge of my battle?
I have wondered if you are dead or alive.
Kiss me again, I have no fear.
Should I see you again a soaring robin I will tear.
Brave your heart and faith you shall have.
Resurrection of the coat giver.
Your love enhanced my shelter.
My belief is, you're alive and you're crying inside.
My visions don't lie, still I love you!

Note: Today inhumane people who deliberately infect
others with Aids can spread the disease without having a
true fear of being caught. They're dying and don't care to
kill others, they're hurting badly. I hear some have been
prosecuted by the law, but is this truly justice when
compared to the number of those who are getting away
with murder! It's a sanctioned disease! May the people
come away from her quickly!!! Who is she?
Ans. The US Government and all who keep quite!

Poor Joseph, the Crying Father of the Immaculate Son

Peace Be Unto You,

Oh, there is my brother Joseph he is crying again.
Sad over this world's greatest sin.
He like many has fathered very precious and outstanding children I gather.
And he like many has fought hard to maintain them baring many tremors.
So many children are snatched away by hands of evil child nabbers, because the authorities are not focused on priorities like our future.
They say Kidnapping but as a compound that means a goat who falls asleep.
For if at once your child let's off his guard he may end up taken from the streets.
Or even worse, hateful and expecting women may trade beds with a bank, hunk, or thug.
But Joseph is one who cannot defend his son. Don't argue just think and search for love!
Joseph has died. His spirit lives on as promised; you laugh!
His spirit is of the righteous so I who strive will speak on his behalf.
And many who are like me will go to war over this spiritually blatant attack.
The Bible was originally written in Hebrew and the Aramaic tongue you take it for fun.

So it's an obvious crime to have changed the name of his great and beloved son; from Isa to Jesus, and other warriors of peace.

So, I must bring up a parable so that all the confusion over who is the father of Jesus shall cease.

There are millions who believe in the lies and treasures sit hidden in closets.

But when Mary and Joseph were searching for their child Jesus, in the Bible the truth was triumphantly recorded.

Go to Luke chapter 2 verses 48 through 52.

Where Jesus did not dispute with his Mother Mary over Joseph being the physical father, so why do you?

He revealed that he had become a prophet and his Father was no more.

But the people were astounded and they pondered till they gathered the score.

Will that be you today and how long will it take?

Before you bring the truth to your ministers and pastors, and bid them a good day!

Oh Joseph, your suffering, your tears will soon fall no more.

I pray the peace of the world is increased, so that all fathers like him will lose their sons no more!

No More, No More! No More!

All who are guilty give back the sons to the fathers. Let the world be free, let the world be free! Allah U Akbar! God Is The Greatest! God Is the Greatest. Amen.

She Walks With The God!

She told them to leave her alone.
She screamed till the pain reached her home.
Here nerves broke her rhythm when they became off set.
And she turned to her supplements that failed her to death.
Her sweat ran a river into a courtroom of shattered wishes.
And the reminder overturned her gaze, her life's regretful
switches.
These are the days. A solo of multiple trails.
When she realized that there was only meant to be one, she
prevailed.
This sister, she knew when the men roared from invisible
trees.
But she did not know the word from the Mountain and
from whom people will flee.
Her troubles won over her heart like silent whispers, from
the wickedly cold, within the deadliest winters and
summers.
She was afraid of the garter but poison was elsewhere, until
she met with the angel that took her "the queen"
outta' there!
"It wasn't me, it was your faith that you survive by, and the
grace of the God", said the Angel on time.
Was the matter decreed?
Yes, she stood firm in heart without wine!
The soldier came to yell at her riding an eagle.
And her days became much shorter, her patience became
feeble.
She remembered her hand was held by "The Son."

And there was no one who could shame her, not by the power of any other one.

For she walked with the God!

She tells the world that she walks with The God!

She told her troubles that she **WALKS WITH THE GOD!**

She stormed through the courtroom doors with the winds of the prophets.

Gently with her book in hand and stated to the principle, "I walk with the God".

Her days have no number now. Her life is complete now.

She has a new father, a new husband, a new brother, a new friend.

She has a new letter, a new guard, and new thing to remember:

"All honors belong to The God!" She would never again leave.

She has become like onto Him, she is Free!

She has become!

She has become!

She has become!

She walks with the God at daytime, and behind the many veils of her so accurate dreams.

Sweet Cookies

This is life; it's a sweet cookie.
It's so good when you know the Lord.
But it's so short, this life.
But is it really, is it really short?

The Lord said that there's more to come.
The Lord of the Worlds said something about....
The Hereafter, that's the over and the start.
The ending for the wicked and beginning for the one of
pure heart.
The love we share as individuals shall break through the
caves and enter the air like Indians charging to free the
slaves.

Is the living the rich, is that all that we care for?
If that's the life that we seek, then our lives are just too
short.
We are the righteous. Yes me, and yes you, let us flee to the
Lord of the Worlds, in Islam (Peace).
It's the Mahdi, the Khalifa, the Son of Man the Great One.
Be Forever Mindful.
He's The Wise one, in whom is the Spirit, and two sides;
one pleasing and other dreadful.
What do you want? What do I want? What does anyone
want? Thou shall not!
For if we do, it will be over like the taste of Sweet,
The Taste of Sweet...

Wait a minute did I hear you heart? See your smile in a
vision? What was that, hear that, just **listen**?
It wasn't just thunder, but a sign of a Master in a Universal
Kitchen,
Cooking what the people wanted, Sweet Cookies!
 Let's go for the Hereafter together, and leave those cookies
alone!

Children Never Ask For Nothing

So what he asked for ice cream, his wishes are simple you
know what I mean.
So what she asked for jump rope, her wishes are simple you
know, you cope!
So what baby cries for bo-bo, baby doesn't want anything,
you already know!
What's it to you? What, how dare you ask me that?
It's my life to be me; it's my life to be me,
That's a father to every child in my very vicinity.
That's a mother to ever child who lost their mommy.
That's me, can't you see that's me!
Your mirror is my mirror if you would join me.
Let's see, cause Children Never Ask for Nothing.
The never ask for nothing, they don't know.
They just love us and the want us to be us so they can
grow.
Children never ask for nothing, the just love us so much.
Can you give yourself the hug that they can conjure up?
So what if she ask you to take her to school,
To be at her 1st show, and don't act a fool.
So what if he asked you to comb his hair.
He should have to ask you say. Why'd you give me that
stare?
So what if she stepped on your foot, and hurt your little toe,
She'd die for you, if you let her mind grow.
Don't tell me, I know, Children Never Ask for Nothing!

Thank you for reading these words, but it means nothing if you continue to allow a child to suffer, but you do if you don't follow these rules. Let's put it this way, are you the type that:

1. Sees a child getting hit in the face by his parent or guardian and doesn't do anything to help.
2. Doesn't care to stop a child from putting his or her hand in filth?
3. Doesn't clean where children play, or iron your baby's clothing when you have the means.
4. Doesn't report indecencies, and turn your head the other way.
5. Doesn't stop them with kind (hard) words when they use the n and b words in public.
6. Doesn't care for children who are not from your womb. Who's doing that?
7. Doesn't care to stop children from talking about fighting each other.
8. Wishes bad things for the children you are too weak to control.
9. Smokes cigarettes or worse right in their faces.
10. Can't keep your pants up with your mate long enough for the child to go to sleep first.
11. Gives your child a beating per bad!
12. Calls your child "Terrible 2's", "Spoiled Brat", or "idiot".
13. Won't stop for a second to tie his or her shoes!

Is that you?

Take Your Hands off Me!

Take your hands of me, yes I hate you.
You say, "God loves everybody, so I should be the same way!"
You can't fool everybody with that talk today.
Everybody doesn't love God, some love him.
But others out there put their hands on me.
They don't love God; they put their hands on me.
They violate the black man, and if they could, well...
You can't say you love God, *Take Your Hands off Me.*
Love is a two way street with no splinters, no off ramps.
You can't take God's Love, then trunk it and leave the car.
You better take it where you go!
Then you got the nerve to put the body of a brother in the trunk where you left the love of God, forgetting.
You better remember God's love wherever you go!
Once you put God to the side, turn your head and put your hands on me, you became a DEVIL, unclean, and hateful.
Take your hands off me, you could be my brother!
Take your hands off me, not you. You know, you know!
Take your hands off me, both of you.
You don't love the original man; you are of your father the Devil who was a liar from the beginning.
My brother Jesus told me that, you are a liar, you are, and you are the oppressor of the poor, the righteous and the unlearned.
What man wrote and what's revealed by God are 2 different things!
You hate God's People don't you?
Take your hands off my family, and take your hands off me!

Brigade salute!!! Stand by…

Stories

SENISTAR ™

Introduction

This story encourages both children and adults to think deeply on the subject of truth and its opposite.

It takes place in the average town, with average folk, who together experience divine intervention in a very interesting fashion to say the least. You like animals?

Enough of this, let's get right to it.

I'm Scared

There was an eight-year-old little sister named Mary who loved to hear stories her parents told at night. She noticed that the stories started to get shorter as she got older and she thought of a way to get her parents to stay with her a bit longer. However, she wasn't very honest.

One night Sister Mary's mother and father told her a great bed time story about the forest and the trees. It was a great story and Mary was so happy you could see the smile on her face grow and grow. Mary, like always, became really sleepy during the neck of the story. Evidence of her great smile started to go away as her eyes shuttered to a close. She was falling asleep. Her father then kissed her on her head to wish her a blessed night. Her mother then said quietly to their daughter, "As-Salaam Alaikum (peace be unto you)" and then they both walked silently to the door.

Suddenly Sister Mary shouted, "Don't' go Mommy and Daddy", with her eyes wide open. Her Father was a bit shocked to see that she was not asleep at all, but still had the strength to wake and call them. He asked her, "what's wrong my little princess? Sister Mary replied, "I'm falling asleep but I'm scared, can you please tell me another story. And while appearing to sob she added, "I'm so afraid". So her father said to her Mom, "Let's tell her another one. She'll soon fall fast asleep". They agreed to tell her one more story. The story was great. It was about a horse and a porcupine that refused to get out of the way so he (the horse) could pass by. Once Mary's eyes shuttered down the father and mother tried to leave and go about their night when suddenly Mary arose again and just before mom turned off the light. Mary shouted, "Daddy please don't leave me, Mommy please". Her mother with surprise in her eyes asked, "my child what's wrong?" Sister Mary replied, "I told you mommy, I'm Scared". Her father became concerned at this point, but knew that Mary was only trying to get them to stay longer and for some reason could not fall asleep. Her mother also figured out that Mary was so interested in their great stories that she wanted to stay up and hear them again and again. Father said to mother, "Let's give her the benefit of the doubt, I'll tell her one more story". Mary said, "Oh thank you father, thanks for understanding".

The two concerned parents both sat on Mary's big bed. Her father prayed and asked Allah (God) to please give him another story and started to tell her a story about a bear and an oak tree. Mary loved the story and her eyes again began to shutter down. Her father and mother started to walk silently to the door. Mary woke up again, shouting louder, and this time more than ever. "Mommy please, Daddy please, don't leave me!" Then the father and mother shouted together at the same time, "what's wrong with you child, have you gone out of your mind?" And Mary said to them silently, "I'm Scared".

Mary's father then explained to her mother that there was no way that he was going to play into this any more. He told his wife, "We will let her fall asleep on her own". So they both kissed her on her cheek, one on either side and told her that they had to go. Mary said, "all right, but I'm so scared". It was no use, the two just walked out the door. Mary's father said to her as he walked away, "You're growing up Mary and it's time you showed us how big of a girl you are". Mary's mother said to her, "Listen to your father Mary, it's true you're growing so tall these days, and into an intelligent princess too". Little Mary started to feel a bit worried that her plan didn't work. They both left the room when suddenly there was a bang on Mary's window "Bang!" Sister Mary shouted, "I'm scared." "Something is there". Unaware that something actually did happen, Mary's father thought she was just acting. Mary's Mother also thought she was acting and decided to ignore her. Then another sound "Bang." Something hit the window. Mary shouted, "I'm scared, I'm scared, I'm scared." "There's trouble".

At this time of the night Mary's father would always go to the store to get a drink of hot chocolate. He liked to walk outside to get a little fresh air and sometimes snap pictures with his digital camera before he went to bed. The store was just a block away. With Mary shouting "I'm scared" he smiled and told his wife, "I'm going to the store; call me on my cell phone if she gets any worse". She replied, "please, there's nothing coming that I can't handle, I'm her mother remember". "And beauty too", he gallantly replied. And so he put on his coat and hat and started out the door. Just as he went past the front lawn he saw something peculiar. It was a squirrel. It was not only wide-awake at an odd hour of the evening, but he was tossing nuts. Mary's father shouted, "Hey you little squirrel, what are you doing?" The squirrel looked at him and stopped what he was doing. It didn't move at all. It just looked at him as if he was happy to see him. Mary's father then startled a bit by the squirrels' reaction, shouted, "You're supposed to be sleeping with the other squirrels at this time. You go on now get!" So the quick squirrel tossed a nut at Mary's window, and her father could hear Mary screaming as she was the whole evening. Mary's father then shouted, "Hey squirrel, want to come with me to the store?" The squirrel ran off into the night. It was as if he was angry that Mary's father was interrupting him in his moment of fun. So Mary's father laughed and went to get his hot chocolate.

Upon his return home he told his wife all about the squirrel. "I know what was bothering our daughter", he said to her. He proceeded to tell her all about the squirrel and of how he was able to toss nuts at terrific heights. They both laughed but silently for about 15 minutes. It was so funny to them. Mary's mother asked as they started to calm down, "I think Mary was fibbing in the beginning, what you think?" Mary's father said, "Sure she was, but Allah (God) sent that squirrel for good reason I'm sure of it, it probably came around the time we left her room". She agreed and smiled, then kissed his cheek. He then said, "I have a surprise for our little wise one, and we must correct her for not being honest, but first I'm going to give her this little surprise". They both went up to her room and there was Sister Mary. She was so scared and really worried, "why did you leave me, why, I told you I was scared. Something was at the window". "What was at the window?" asked her mother. She answered, "I don't know mom." "Maybe a robber and it could have been a bad man". So her father then sat on her bed and smiled at his wife, and she returned with a smile to him. Sister Mary said, "What are you two smiling about. This is not funny, there was something there scaring me". Mary's father said, "Surprise!" Mary looked puzzled. Mary's father was wise to carry that small digital camera with him wherever he went and while he was talking to the squirrel he happened to get some pictures of him as he was tossing the nuts at Mary's window. He showed Mary the photos that were brilliantly captured and displayed on the screen of his camera. Mary looked at them and asked, "Father what's this. Is that a squirrel?" He replied to her, "yes it is, and do you know what this squirrel is doing in this picture, and can you tell exactly what is he doing Mary?" She replied, "Not really, it looks like he's dancing father. What's that in his little hand? Is it a nut?" Her mother replied, "Yes it is

Mary. Your father took that picture just a few minutes ago right outside the house behind your window." Mary's father then said, "Mary are you hearing us? Do you know what's going on now, and what you seem to be so scared of? Are you getting the picture?" Mary said, "No, all I know is I was scared and someone was trying to get in my room". Her father then told her, "it was the squirrel my child. I took these pictures as he was tossing nuts in our back yard right behind you're window." Mary said, "I can't believe that. Squirrels don't toss nuts. They store them, they eat them, but they don't play dodge ball". "Ha, Ha" He said, "Yes that's true but this squirrel was a bit different. First of all he was up at the time when most squirrels are sleeping and he was in fact not scared of me at all. In fact, he was tossing nuts out there all over the lawn". Mary started to feel bad inside and her head went down in a bit of sorrow because she knew that this squirrel was not the reason why this started at all. The time it took to explain the actions of their new furry visitor by her father weighed heavy on her conscious as the truth would have taken less effort to expose. Her father then asked her, "Mary, are you scared now? Are you scared of squirrels, because this is the man that was trying to get into your house? It was a male squirrel". Her mother then gave her a hug, but spoke firmly into her ear, "the next time you tell us the truth, and never lie again to your Mommy and Daddy". She said, "I know, I'm sorry, I really just wanted…" Her father stopped her and said, "We know my child. You wanted us to tell you more stories, but I have to ask you again. Don't ever lie to me again please?" He then asked his daughter, "Sweetheart, do you realize that it was Allah (God) who sent that squirrel to help us to teach you that there is no way for us in lying? No squirrel would be tossing nuts at this time of night. It had to be Allah's (God's) doing, a special lesson just for you". Mary's mother then said, "You are a special child Mary that Allah (God) would take the time to teach you and help us. Be sure to honor Allah (God) that you will always tell the truth from now on". "You'll honor us, your parents", she added.

Mary fell asleep. Her father said, "Is she asleep now for real?" Indeed Sister Mary had finally fallen asleep. Mary's father and mother left the room and started to chat. "You know that Allah (God) appeared in the person of a little friendly squirrel to her on this night to teach her a lesson of truth", said her father to her mother. She replied sharply, "Don't you dare play around like that; Allah (God) wasn't the squirrel". "But my dear wife, he wasn't scared of me. It didn't run. It could have been God", he said. "Oh, boy, here we go, spooky island, the land of wild imaginations, little sleep and *HEY BOSS THE SQUIRREL, THE SQUIRREL*", she said jokingly. "You don't really mean that", he replied. With wise words she responded, "No, my dear husband Allah (God) wouldn't enter the body of the squirrel as he would a man. He only needs to tell it what to do and it will respond. He works through the squirrel and may have trained and commanded the squirrel to toss the nuts at our baby's window". "That's it; you could be our towns' first woman minister. Let's go to bed now", he replied. She was pleased by his words. They soon feel fast asleep after thanking the Allah (God) for His intervention on this trying night.

The end…

Thank you for reading these words! I wonder where that squirrel is now. "Bang!" Hey, what was that?

Stories continued...

SENISTAR ™

Introduction

This story is for all to read and discuss amongst themselves. Picture this one like TV's own CSI or Law and Order, its practical and based on many facts.

It was on Sunday, February 18, 2007 after having told this as a bed time story that I started to write this. It's inspired by actual events of my life. Before you read this you must know that I have never been on the city of Allah (God), better known as the Mother Ship (or Ezekiel's Wheel). Nor have I flown in a Baby Plane, better known as a so-called UFO. Yes, I do believe in the existence of the Air-Force of the Nation of Islam here in the wilderness of North America (under the direction of The Honorable Minister Farrakhan Muhammad, who is lead, by The Most Honorable Elijah Muhammad). The (the so-called UFO's) hovered over Central Park during my first ever sight of them in 1995. They are simply magnificent!

I use the name "Ishmael" in the story because I believe (if it's the will of Allah) the day will come where my spiritual brother, Minister Ishmael Muhammad will see his father again who is in my opinion very much alive and well (ref. *Is it Possible that the Honorable Elijah Muhammad Is Still Physically Alive, by Jabril Muhammad*). I dedicate this portion of the book to him for all the good work he has done on behalf of our people, in the good name of his father, the Most Honorable Elijah Muhammad.

I dedicate it also to whom I believe to be the long awaited Son of Man, and Great Mahdi, whom I revere as my father-Master Fard Muhammad- to whom all praises are due forever!

SENISTAR ™

Brother Ishmael's meets the Messenger

Deep in the heart of Harlem during the 1990's at Muhammad Mosque No.7 there were 2 brothers. One named Brother Ishmael and the other named Brother Peter. Now Brother Ishmael was a kind soul of a young man, always helping the M.G.T (women of the Nation of Islam, **M**uslim **G**irls in **T**raining) with their bags and never doubting the word of any Believer. He was of the best **F**ruit **of I**slam (men of the Nation of Islam, F.O.I.) ever in the history of the Mosque. His kindness and dedication surely made him stand out as a Top Soldier as they say of the best of the men at the Mosque. Brother Peter was very strange however. He was a bit short circuited; nice one day and deceitful the next, happy one day then angry the next. Needless to say Brother Peter was a bit rebellious. Despite this, Brother Ishmael was such a good brother he befriended Brother Peter. He saw goodness in every one at the Mosque and even when it wasn't much, he still treated everyone with the greatest showing of sincere consideration.

One day Brother Ishmael and Brother Peter were walking together down 126th Street near the back of the world famous Apollo Theatre when suddenly a Baby Plane (a so-called UFO) silver and glowing with lights appeared over their heads. Brother Ishmael was the first to spot the Baby Plane and said, with all his heart and strength in his lungs, "Look Brother Peter, Look, Allah U Akbar, Allah U Akbar, Allah U Akbar (God is the greatest)". It was a wonder how no one but Brother Peter heard him. Brother Peter then looked at Brother Ishmael as he pointed to the Baby Plane. Brother Peter just stood in amazement and said nothing at first. Then Brother Ishmael said, "Do you see it Brother Peter; it's a Baby Plane, it's a Baby Plane?" Brother Peter then said, "Yes, I see it, wow!" (While he stood there he was shivering in fear). Brother Ishmael said to him as he noticed that Brother Peter was frightened, "Don't worry. That's our family in that wheel there in the sky". The Baby Plane started to move to the left, and then it stopped. Brother Ishmael shouted, "Allah U Akbar, did you see that Brother Peter? It moved". Brother Ishmael was a great brother of faith. He then started to speak at the people or person in the wheel, He said, "As-Salaam Alaikum (peace be unto you), dear family in the little wheel. Would you move again for us? Can you please move to the right now?" The Baby Plane then moved to the right. Brother Ishmael said, "All praises are due to Allah (God), did you see that Brother Peter?" Brother Peter then replied, "oh yeah, it moved all right". Then suddenly as they both stood in amazement a great stream of lights started to blare from the little wheel in the sky as it moved from side to side. Then it vanished while traveling at terrific speeds upwards to the heavenly Harlem sky. Brother Ishmael was so happy, "Brother Peter", he whispered placing his arm over Peters shoulders with tears in his eyes, "Do you realize when something like that happens what we must do? Do you realize how significant this is? Do you know that Allah (God) loves us"? Brother Peter with a strange look in his eye said nothing. He just walked with Brother Ishmael back to the Mosque but said nothing all the way back to the Mosque which was on 5th Avenue several blocks away. Brother Ishmael said, "I wonder if anyone else saw it?" He looked around as they were walking away and saw no one on the block. Brother Peter still kept silent and never responded to him as they walked to the Mosque.

It was at night, F.O.I. (Fruit of Islam) class, and it seemed that all the brothers were in front of the Mosque waiting for the doors to open to be let in. Brother Ishmael stood across the street with Brother Peter and shouted, "I can't wait to tell them, they are going to be so happy to know". Brother Peter remained silent as they walked across the street and met with the others who were very happy to see them both. "Brother Ishmael, As-Salaam Alaikum (peace be unto you)", said one brother. Brother Ishmael replied, "Walaikum Salaam (and Peace to You) brothers". That's when Brother Peter stood far from Brother Ishmael. Brother Ishmael couldn't hold it in at all. He just came out and said, "Brothers I saw a Baby Plane, it was right over the Apollo Theater". One brother said, "When, Brother Ishmael, when did you see it?" Brother Ishmael replied, "Just now, it was beautiful and it moved for us. I just asked the brother who flew it to move the wheel from where I stood and it moved to the right just as I asked". All the brothers in front of the Mosque started to crowd around Brother Ishmael with smiles on their faces and were happy to hear of Brother Ishmael's experience and wanted to hear more. Then Brother Ishmael turned to see if Brother Peter was there. He couldn't see him at first because Brother Peter was trying to walk away. That's when Brother Ishmael shouted, "Brother Peter saw it. Isn't that right Brother Peter? He was right with me when it happened, Brother Peter, tell them". Brother Peter responded, "Brother's crazy, I don't know what he's talking about" The brothers were perplexed and amazed at his reply.

It was hard enough for the brothers to grasp that a Baby Plane would appear over the World Famous Apollo Theatre and even more so, move when Brother Ishmael asked the driver of the Baby Plane to move. But when Brother Peter called it all off as if Brother Ishmael was a big fluke that was enough to make most of them disbelieve in his claim. It was sad to see for those who really believed Brother

Ishmael. They were too few against the many that started to walk away in suspicion, and in doubt.

As the Mosque doors opened and they all went upstairs together. As Brother Ishmael was walking up the stairs he could hear the brothers who now disbelieved laughing and mocking at him, "baby planes over the Apollo Theatre, for what, to beam up the Sand Man, Ha, Ha, Ha", said one brother. "I knew Kee-Kee and the Sand Man was the same person, or they probably switch up in a UFO, you never see them together", said another while laughing. Brother Ishmael was furious at Brother Peter, but remained calm. He didn't say much to Brother Peter who was near him walking up the stairs at about 2 steps behind him. He just turned around and gave him a hard cold look. This was bad for Brother Ishmael, so it seemed. His credibility was shattered and only Allah (God) could save him from being ousted for the majority of the brotherhood was not sure of him anymore.

Later that night, after class, Brother Ishmael started to cry. He was in his room at his mother's home where he lived. He couldn't believe that he had no way of overcoming the attack on his character, which was twisted by the lie of his Brother Peter. "I always knew he was suspect and strange", Brother Ishmael said to himself of Brother Peter. Brother Ishmael was such a good brother he prayed for Brother Peter that Allah (God) would forgive him for the evil that he had committed against him. For he knew that Allah (God) would severely chastise him for such a lie. Brother Peter continued to pray, "Oh Allah (God) please tell me why you have forsaken me. Is this a punishment? Why did that brother tell such a lie my reputation is ruined? Please answer me?" asked Brother Ishmael to Allah (God). After Brother Ishmael finished praying, he wasn't very sad anymore. He just went right to sleep. That night there was a deep fog and the streets were so covered with it that even the cars had to drive extremely slow for there was next to zero visibility. You couldn't see a thing in front of you at all. Some drivers stopped completely in the streets and took to diners and hotels for the night. It was one of the foggiest nights of the century and the newspaper personnel were out to press the story of "The Greatest Fog".

Meanwhile, back at Brother Peter's house, he was biting his nails in a reckless manor nearly tearing the skin off his fingers in fear. He knew that what he saw was real, but he was too weak of a man to bear witness and stand with Brother Ishmael. This brother was what we call a hypocrite. He "believes" only when it's to his own benefit and when he is comfortable. His self-accusing spirit (better known as the guilty conscious) was pounding him in the head. He was ashamed of himself, but made no plans to right the wrong that he had just committed against good brother Ishmael or to Allah (God) and the brother who flew the Baby Plane. However, he planned to work hard for Allah (God), but that wasn't going to get him off the hook in Allah's (God's) sight. "I'm going to knock on all the doors in Harlem and get everyone to come to the Mosque", said Brother Peter to himself. "They'll soon make me an officer and I'll work harder than everyone" he continued to promise himself." He even prayed. However, Allah (God) was not pleased with him!

Back at Brother Ishmael's he woke up in the middle of the night. He had a vision. He saw another Baby Plane in his vision. It was almost as if it was real. That's what made him wake up. "Wow, I can't believe it! That Baby Plane in my dream; it looked just like the one we saw today in the back of the Apollo", said Brother Ishmael to himself. He got out of his bed and went to drink some water; he even splashed some on his face while in the kitchen to see if he was not still dreaming. (Splash) "I'm real", he said loud like a riff from James Brown. Then he laughed to himself, "Ha, ha, ha, I'm really having a night of power here on this day!" But Brother Ishmael was still very tired and soon as he finished his water he went right back to sleep. When Brother Ishmael woke up the next morning he was in a strange place. He was on the "mother ship" where all the Baby Planes dock. The wheel where Allah (God) and His Christ now live! The mother wheel of the Teachings of the Most Honorable Elijah Muhammad; it was THE GREAT CITY IN THE SKY!

Brother Ishmael awoke in terror, "Ahhh, Allah U Akbar, Allah U Akbar, Allah U Akbar". He couldn't stop saying that *God is the Greatest* as he was frightened nearly to death. Then a voice came over him and said, "Be still my brother. It's okay". Brother Ishmael recognized the voice, but at first he couldn't make it out. It was a gentle voice. It made Brother Ishmael feel good. It was the voice of the Messenger; the Honorable Elijah Muhammad. Brother Ishmael, like most dedicated F.O.I., would not mistake such a unique voice. The Messenger sounded just like he did when he was on Mother Asia (Earth) amongst the Believers (Members of the Mosque), and Brother Ishmael was a good student of the Messengers Teachings. He listened to every tape he could find. He knew the voice of his Messenger. The Messenger spoke again, "Dearest Brother Ishmael, be not worried. You are on the Mother Ship". Brother Ishmael, then started to cry as he replied, "Is that you dear Holy Apostle? Is this really you I hear?" The Messenger answered, "yes, and fear not for you are safe with me here my dear student. I love you". "Brother Ishmael said, "Where are you? I can't see you". The

Messenger replied, "Soon you will, but for now be calm and look around. I'll be sending a guide to meet you. He's a good brother just like you". The Messenger's voice went away. Brother Ishmael was feeling stronger now. He was beginning to cope. He felt safe and he started to smile. He said, "Allah U Akbar (God is the greatest)," but this time it was with a joyful tone. He wasn't scared anymore.

Brother Ishmael put his hand on the floor. "Is this gold?" he said. Then he touched the walls, "silver" he said, and then he looked all around as he stood in a room made of precious metals. Of such he never laid his eyes on before. It looked like gold and silver, but the shine was so unique that it had to be of the finest grade he had ever seen. Of course he was in the City of Allah (God). Suddenly there was an opening in the wall and without any sound a brother appeared in a fine silk like suite. It was woven in gold and very new to the eye. The brother's eyes were very dark and mysterious looking, but Brother Ishmael still could feel the warmth of his spirit. His skin was also very dark. He was an original man like Brother Ishmael. Brother Ishmael said, "As-Salaam Alaikum (peace be unto you)". He was always the first to greet brothers back at the Mosque on Asia (Earth), just like the Holy Prophet Muhammad (PBUH) and this time he beat this newly found brother to it. This new brother said, "Walaikum Salaam (and Peace to You), Brother Ishmael. I am here to show you around by the permission of Allah's (God's) Messenger who sends the greetings to you." Brother Ishmael replied, "Thank you dear brother and please return the greetings to him for me. And your skin it looks so smooth. I hope you don't mind my saying so, but there's not a mark on you". The new Brother replied, "The only mark on me is the Sun, the Moon, and the Star." You understand?" Brother Ishmael said, "oh yes, Islam (Peace), you're my kind of brother.

What's your name? What shall I call you?" The new brother said with a smile and gleam in his eyes, "my name is also Brother Ishmael". They both laughed and smiled at each other. "The Messenger was right", said the new Brother Ishmael as he continued. "You know that's why I was chosen to be your escort and guide throughout the Mother Ship. The Messenger told me that you would be more comfortable because my name is the same as yours. Now I see why by your reaction". "That's true. It has made me feel good to know that we have so much in common", said Brother Ishmael. The new Brother Ishmael replied, "The Honorable Elijah Muhammad is always 100 percent right and exact. I'm glad you feel comfortable and I know that looking at me is amazing to see. But soon you will look the same, so get used to it". "What?" asked Brother Ishmael. "Don't you act like you don't know what I'm talking about Brother Ishmael. You know the Teachings. You know that Master Fard Muhammad will cause you to grow a new growth. You read this," said the new Brother Ishmael to him. "Oh yes, so this is what I will look like huh (he touched the new brothers forearm), but I'll look even more handsome I bet", said Brother Ishmael. "Funny brother, now come with me. Let me show you throughout the city. It's your home too you know", said the new Brother Ishmael.

They both walked together as the new Brother Ishmael took hold of Brother Ishmael's hand and they sort of floated. It was so amazing of an experience for both of them. Never before did the new Brother Ishmael get to speak to a brother from the surface of Asia (Earth) and never before did Brother Ishmael experience a tour on the actual Mother Plane, which he read of in the Messenger's books; "Message to the Blackman in America" and "Our Saviour

Has Arrived". It was fun but, the real fun was yet to be experienced.

They came to a room which had a round door. Brother Ishmael was wide eyed and asked with a loud voice, "What's this place?" The new Brother Ishmael replied, "Please shhhhh... This is your room brother". "WHAT" replied Brother Ishmael? "Did you say my room?" "Yes, all you have to do is say your name *QUIETLY* and the door will open", said the new brother. So Brother Ishmael said his name, "Ishmael", and the door opened and withdrew straight into the ceiling. There were no hinges at all either. A light shinned from the room as they both walked in. The new Brother had to give Brother Ishmael a friendly little push to get him started. "Why did you push me like that", asked Brother Ishmael? "Because, if I waited for you we would still be in the hallway. Come on now let me show you your room", said the new Brother Ishmael as he chuckled. They both walked in and Brother Ishmael couldn't keep his mouth closed. He was asking about everything (What's this? what's that?). Before the new brother could answer a question Brother Ishmael would ask another. It was a landslide Q&A if you ever heard one. But all that stopped at this final question, "Is that what I think it is?" said Brother Ishmael. Right before their eyes stood a hovering ship within the room. It was silver and had soft lights blaring from it. The lights didn't hurt their eyes when they looked at them and they were very large as well. "Yes, that's a baby plane", replied the new Brother Ishmael in response to his question. "Wow", said Brother Ishmael. "How did you get that in here?" he continued. "Well that's not hard. I'll show you, but first I must tell you that this is your Baby Plane", said the New Brother Ishmael. "You can't be serious. My own baby plane", as tears started to roll from his eyes. Brother Ishmael started to cry. "Brother don't cry. It's a gift from Master Fard Muhammad, the Son of Man. He wanted me to tell you that He loves you and that He will see you soon", said the new Brother Ishmael. Brother Ishmael couldn't help it because he was overwhelmed at the words which the New Brother spoke; it took a few minutes for him to get his thoughts together to speak. The new brother put his arms around him and gave him a great hug. This hug was so energetic. The spirit of Allah (God) was strong in them both. As they hugged atoms of light sparked around them. As soon as Brother Ishmael noticed the sparkling atoms of light, he stopped crying and stood in shock. "I don't know brother. This sure is a trip", said Brother Ishmael, referring to the lights he saw floating around him. "Don't worry that happens all the time here. Wait until you see what happens when everyone gets together", said the new Brother Ishmael. "Everyone, like whom?" asked Brother Ishmael. "You'll see, but not today", said the new brother. "What is this ship like inside? Can I go in it? Did you did say it was mine?" Brother Ishmael said. "Yes you may go in, but you must be careful. I must warn you. You'll be driving it today if you are careful," said the new Brother Ishmael. "What, I can't even ride a skateboard, what do you mean I'll be driving it? I'm not driving that anywhere. Are you crazy brother? Have you lost your mind? Look at me", said Brother Ishmael. The new Brother Ishmael turned towards him and said, "I am going to leave you now. Go on inside and you'll see it's not hard. When you get in there you'll be flying within minutes. You're a natural". "Are you crazy? I'm going to report you to the Messenger! You must be nuts. I'll look at it, but I'm not flying that anytime soon. I need training or something," said Brother Ishmael. "No you don't. You'll see. I was like you when I started to drive my very own Baby Plane. I was a little boy then and even at the age of 12 I was able to drive it with the aid of my father who was beside me", replied the new Brother Ishmael. They talked for a while about the wheel, but the new brother didn't give Brother Ishmael too much to go on, not much at all. But it wasn't like he didn't want to teach him of his new toy. He knew that Brother Ishmael would not need much teaching at all. These planes were made for the divine man.

After a few minutes of conversation the new brother left Brother Ishmael and promised to return in 20 minutes. "I'll be back in twenty minutes and by the time I get back you would have already flown your baby plane. This I am sure of", said the new brother as he walked away. "As-Salaam Alaikum (peace be unto you) my brother from the surface of Asia (Earth), I'll see you in 20 minutes," he added. Then the Guide walked away as Brother Ishmael returned the greetings.

Brother Ishmael stood there in shock. Here he was in front of a huge baby plane in his own room on the Mother Ship. Brother Ishmael started to ramble back and forth and said to himself, "What on earth is going on? This brother just walked out of the room and left me by myself. On top of that he thinks I'm going to fly this thing. He's out of his mind!" But soon enough, Brother Ishmael became quite curious and surveyed closer. He touched the plane gently with his right hand. "Oh, this is cool", he said. "Ishmael", he said. He remembered how he got into the room and an opening was revealed as a light came down from the Baby Plane and engulfed him. Within a second he was inside the Baby Plane. "Ahhh", he exhaled, in amazement. He was inside the cockpit of the plane right at the foot of the controls. Needless to say, this brother was in total shock again! Then a beautiful voice came though the speaker system of the plane. It sounded like a woman, but heavenly computerized. *The reverb and flange effect was superior as expected, after all this was a baby plane.* "AS-SALAAM ALAIKUM (peace be unto you)," said the voice. "Who's that?" shouted Brother Ishmael. There was silence. Then Brother Ishmael said, "Walaikum Salaam (and peace to you)," but he didn't know who or what he was talking to. He remembered that it was customarily sound to respond to the universal greeting of Islam regardless to who greets you with these words. Suddenly the control lights turned on and so did a motor from within. The plane started to get warm. "Hey, what's going on in here? Who's doing that?" said Brother Ishmael. He then sat down in the seat. He knew that this was going to be the experience of his life. He wasn't so scared at first, but soon he was going to be scared again for sure. The voice returned, "Where would you like to go?" said the voice in the Baby Plane. "I'm not going anywhere?" "Who's that?" "What is this?" "Are you some sort of auto pilot?" asked Brother Ishmael. "Yes, I am your Automatic Guide and Transport Aid. My name is Khadijah. You can change my name if you like", she said. "That's okay, Brother Ishmael responded. What did you mean where would I like to go? I don't know a thing about driving this plane. Besides my newly found brother said he'd be back in 20 Minutes. We don't have time to go anywhere. We're in the middle of space", said Brother Ishmael to the voice in the plane. "Where would you like to go? We can travel at the terrific speed of one hundred miles per second?" asked Khadijah. "One hundred miles per second, that's insane. I'm not trying to go there. That's nuts", said Brother Ishmael. But suddenly a thought came to Brother Ishmael and he started to like the idea that he could travel in the plane after his idea started to manifest. He then asked, "Can we go to Harlem?" "Yes, where would you like to go in Harlem of Asia?" asked Khadijah. "I'd like to go to the Mosque. It's Tuesday night and it's the right night. The brother's are there at around 7:00 p.m. eating bean soup. What time is it?" asked Brother Ishmael. "Its 6:45 PM eastern time on Asia (Earth). Would you like to go?" asked Khadijah. Brother Ishmael was truly on the path which the new brother had predicted. Soon he would be a brave soul that he never imagined in his life. "Brother Ishmael, I asked, would you like to go to Muhammad Mosque No.7 in Harlem now?" Khadijah repeated. "Wait a minute, not so fast", said Brother Ishmael. "Can I help? What's wrong? Are you not comfortable?" asked Khadijah. "No, I'm not, you're talking about traveling at speeds of over one hundred miles per second and on top of that I don't see any seat belts on this seat", said Brother Ishmael who was awfully security minded. "There is no need for seat belts. The chair has a more advanced method of safety, but if you would like to go to Harlem and return within the time frame of 20 minutes, which we have now only 15, we will have to leave now. There's no time to explain," said Khadijah. "Okay, let's go", said Brother Ishmael with a timid voice. "You will have to reply with more confidence. Are you certain? Master Fard Muhammad has programmed me to ascertain your sincerity. You don't sound sure," said Khadijah. "I'm sure. I admit it's a first for me, but by the grace of All Mighty Allah (God) I trust what He has prepared for me. I love Master Fard. I know He wouldn't harm me. Let's go to the Mosque now", said Brother Ishmael. "Sit down, we'll be there in a second", said Khadijah. "What, one second, and you don't need seat belts, THAT'S CRAZY", shouted Brother Ishmael. "Countdown, 10, 9, 8, 7, 6, 5..." started Khadijah. "Oh, Allah", Brother Ishmael said, and he continued to pray. Within seconds they were off in flight. The plane flew in a way that wouldn't frighten brother and they were flying so fast that he didn't have time to react. He nearly passed out, but didn't have time even for that. Within seconds they were over 2033 East 125th Street, at Muhammad Mosque No.7.

"WOOAH", said Brother Ishmael, "that was fast. I didn't even feel it. I'm not dizzy and I'm not dead, whew" as he touched each portion of his face with his hands. He didn't even miss his ears. "I'm running a routine check on the atmosphere and areas for disturbances so please stand by. You are above the Mosque now", said Khadijah. Suddenly a window opened (like a shade retracts) and Brother Ishmael could see the Mosque. They were about 100-200 feet above it. No one noticed the baby plane. It was cloaked. "Why can't they see us", asked Brother Ishmael (speaking of the brothers and sisters who were in front of the Mosque and other passerby's). "Well, Brother Ishmael we have a cloaking mechanism. It's activated so that no one can see us but others from the Mother Ship", said Khadijah. "Can we take it off for a minute", asked Brother Ishmael. "It's possible. I have permission from Master Fard Muhammad", said Khadijah. "He's talking to you right now?" asked Brother Ishmael. Khadijah replied, "Yes". "Well, then, turn it off, let them see us for one minute and move around when they do just a little", said Brother Ishmael. "The veil is deactivated", said Khadijah. There were 2 brothers on outside post that noticed the plane first. One shouted, "Look!" There were at least 15 believers out front who all looked up in amazement at the awesome baby plane. "They can see us. Okay, now move", ordered Brother Ishmael to Khadijah. The plane started to move to the right and then to the left. It made a circle around the Mosque and stopped at the same location from whence it started. The people were astounded and started to point. Even passerby's who didn't know anything of such a phenomenal aircraft saw the beautiful baby plane. Brother Ishmael's ears started to ring very hard all of the sudden. "My ears are ringing", he said. "The Master?" asked Khadijah. "Oh, we have to get back", said Brother Ishmael. Khadijah replied, "Say no more". Within seconds they were back in the room on the great and dreadful Mother Ship. "Now I know that you're not an ordinary baby plane. I've never seen anything like you. You must be a new concept plane or something. How did you do that?" asked Brother Ishmael. Then the beam of light that took him up into the baby plane appeared again. It took him out and within seconds, he stood before his new brother Ishmael. "It's you, As-Salaam Alaikum (peace be unto you), this is a real trip Brother Ishmael", said Brother Ishmael to his newly found brother from the Mother Ship. "Would you like something to drink? The tour isn't over yet. There's more to see here on the Wheel Brother Ishmael. After all, this is a city in the sky just as you have read of in the scriptures", said the new Brother Ishmael. "Sure, I'll have whatever you'll have; water, juice, whatever, tea even", said Brother Ishmael. "Tea is fine", said the new Brother Ishmael. They sat in the room as Brother Ishmael told him of his experience of flight on his new baby plane. They laughed and talked for about an hour, building on mathematics, high science, and also scripture. There was no idle talk ever on the Mother ship, as this was strictly enforced. "It's getting late. Let's take a walk to the farm", said the new Brother to Ishmael. "Farm, are you serious?" asked Brother Ishmael. "Yes brother, let's take a walk," said the new brother. And before Brother Ishmael could get the smile off his face, they walked out to the farm. He was astonished at what he saw. There were new animals that he had never seen before, animals that had their own dialect and were extremely intelligent. They even played board games while sitting at small tables. Brother Ishmael couldn't believe his eyes. He was on the Mother Ship for real! It was finally hitting him in his conscious very hard and he started to cry again. The new brother consoled him again and again. With every touch of a new animal Brother Ishmael cried. He cried tears of joy and pure happiness, but his journey on the wheel had to come to an end after this walk to the new farm. He knew he had to go back to Asia (Earth) and when the new brother told him he wasn't sad or shocked. His ears were still ringing also. "It's time to go back to your room Brother Ishmael and then you can get some rest", said the new brother.

On the way back to the room the new found brothers talked some more. "Brother, I'm so happy to have experienced this glimpse of the heaven", said Brother Ishmael. "I know you call it a glimpse because you are aware that you have to return to Asia (Earth)", said the new brother. "How do you know, can you read my thoughts?" asked Brother Ishmael. "All of us on the wheel can read each other's thoughts, but when it's private we don't do that, we have strong love, as well as a respect for your privacy", replied the new brother. "The punishment is death for any violators and is automatically blocked when it's private. You'll get to understand how it works. This head of yours is a radio. You've read of it", added the new brother. When they got back to the room there was a bag of clothing on the chair. Brother Ishmael looked inside the bag after asking permission as it was then granted by the new brother. "It's your pajamas from home on the surface of Asia (Earth)", said the new brother. "Why are they here?" asked Brother Ishmael. "After you take your shower in the bath, you must put them on. Then you will fall asleep and awake back on Asia (Earth) in your house". "What? Are you serious, I have to leave now?" asked Brother Ishmael. "Yes, I thought you knew. Now go in that room (as he pointed to a green door). There you will find the shower", said the new Brother Ishmael. So Brother Ishmael went into the room, but before he could get any further he shouted, "Brother, can you please come here?" His new brother ran to the room where the shower was and asked, "What's wrong Brother Ishmael". "Where's the shower in here?" he asked. The new brother started to laugh. This room was golden and there were knobs but Brother Ishmael wasn't aware at all. "I'm sorry, I should have told you how to operate this", said the new brother. "All you have to do is say the words, but first you must take all your clothing off and place it in this bucket." said the new brother. "What words?" asked Brother Ishmael. "Let me step out first, then I'll tell you," said the new brother. So he stepped out and said, "When you have disrobed I'll tell you the words". So Brother Ishmael prepared himself. However, he was not prepared for what was about to happen. "I'm ready", he said to the new brother as he stood alone in the strange room. "Okay, now when you say these words water will come down like a waterfall on Asia (Earth). You'll feel like you're in a washing machine but a whole lot better. If you need soap, just say "soap." If you need shampoo just say "shampoo." The room has been programmed to reply to English, but when you return you will have to learn Arabic", said the new Brother Ishmael. "Really, that's funny okay, shower", said Brother Ishmael. Then the water came down gently at first, but it was too light of a drizzle for Brother Ishmael. "How do you make it rain harder in here?" he shouted to the new brother. "All you have to say is the word thunder", said the new Brother Ishmael. "Okay, thunder", and the loud sound of thunder exploded as huge amounts of water came down upon him like a real thunderstorm. It wasn't windy though, just lots of water. Brother Ishmael loved it to say the least, to the new brother's amazement. He was actually playing a prank, but he didn't' know that Brother Ishmael likes to live on the wild side sometime. He's from Harlem, you know, *"Go uptown, go uptown!"* He could have said "Light rain", and the computer is programmed to know these commands. It has a most advanced fashion of detection. "Are you okay in there?" asked the new brother. "For sure brother, this is hot. I love it", said, Brother Ishmael. Brother Ishmael then started to play around. All of the sudden the shower shut off. "What's going on?" shouted Brother Ishmael. "You can't use slang in there, didn't you read the Messengers teachings where he said we were never to use baby language? The system shut down, it's a safety measure. You said the words, - this is hot - and the computer didn't understand. It thought it was doing something wrong, so to protect you it shut down." explained the new brother Ishmael to his confused brother. "Oh", Brother Ishmael replied. "Oh, you don't understand, if you keep making mistakes like that the guards will come, they are Death Angels", warned the new brother Ishmael. "You mean like the ones who guard the fire. I don't want any trouble. I read about them in the Holy Quran." said Brother Ishmael. "Don't worry just be very careful in there, no more street talk, okay?" asked the new brother. "Okay, but it's not going to be easy, but I'll do my best. [*Little did they know. Elijah and Master Fard Muhammad the Son of Man were looking at them through an aquarium of water in his chambers. The Messenger chuckled at that one. "That sure was funny", said Elijah.*] Now when is this shower coming back..?" asked Brother Ishmael. And before he could finish the water burst back onto his body. Brother Ishmael was startled a bit but that didn't stop him, he went back to playing again. He said the word "lightening" about 30 times and was in awe over the colors of light that he experienced as well as the mind blowing sounds of thunder. It was the shower of a life time. "How do you stop it?" asked Brother Ishmael. The new brother shouted through the wall again and said, "Just say, Allah U Akbar stop". So he said it, "Allah U Akbar, stop", and the water stopped. Afterwards the room automatically dries in an astonishing method of great speed involving air pressure as towels appeared via levitation for his body. Brother Ishmael was on cloud nine as they say. After all of this it was not hard for him to fall asleep when it was time.

After the shower, the new brother told Brother Ishmael that he would experience much upon his return but to fear nothing but Allah (God). Brother Ishmael's ears continued to ring hard. It was getting late so they made prayer together before the new Brother left his room to allow him to get his much needed rest. "I want you to know that this was of the greatest meeting of my life Brother Ishmael", said the new brother, "I'll never forget this", he added. Then he bid him peace and left the room.

Brother Ishmael went to his bed and said an additional prayer. Right beside his bed was a new book he had never seen before. It was green like the Holy Quran and the pages were written in Arabic, but it was a book like no other he had ever laid his eyes on. The moment he touched the book the spirit of truth came over his flesh. It was electrical in nature and his hairs stood firmly upright. The ringing in his ear increased and he became a bit uncomfortable. However, he was happy because this was all very new to him. As the night grew older he became more interested in the new found book, but he couldn't read Arabic so this made him very tired. He covered himself in the silk blankets and started to rest.

When Brother Ishmael awoke, there was his mother with a doctor from across the hall. "My baby up", said his mother. "As-Salaam Alaikum (peace be unto you) he said.

"You were asleep for hours. We thought you were sick or something". "Thank God he's all right", said her friend the doctor. "I never seen such a case of tiredness in my entire career as a doctor," she added. "I was in another world," said Brother Ishmael with a smile as he alluded.   The doctor then left and things went back to normal at his home.   His mother was quite concerned, but she wasn't worried. "Would you like something to eat?" she asked. "Mother I'd love some bean soup if you have any, and thank you", said Brother Ishmael. "I have plenty and if you'd like I'll through in some more vegetables, because you really need some energy in light of all the sleep you just had", said his mother. "Yes, I'll have all the love you can come up with mom", he said. "Are you alright?" she asked. "Yes, I'm okay, I just am happy to be alive. All praises are due to Allah (God)", he said.

Now as the days passed, Brother Ishmael had so many things to think about. He prayed and watched many speeches of the Honorable Minister Farrakhan Muhammad. Not many believers can say they have spoken to Elijah and recently at that. He was eager to go to the Mosque on Friday to attend study group.   All though he had experienced such a phenomenon, he was still the same Brother Ishmael. He had to learn many lessons of life and he was about to learn one of the toughest ever if he but knew.

When Friday came he was so excited. He dressed in his best suit because he was eager to hear what the believers were going to say about the baby plane they saw. He was the first at the Mosque at around 6:30 pm. He took post in the front and waited until he was received by a lieutenant. After having gone through the check post where all visitors and personnel are searched before entering, he hung up his coat and picked up his Supreme Wisdom and Closing the Gap books. He rushed to the Study Group circle, which was already in progress. When he got there the discussion was on the Mother Ship. How ironic and appropriate this was as they all were witnesses of the Baby Plane, which hovered over the Mosque during last Tuesday's Family night. The Minister of the circle that night was Sister Asst. Minister Melissa Muhammad. When Brother Ishmael sat down in the circle the question was asked of him from her, "Brother Ishmael glad to see you today, As-Salaam Alaikum (peace be unto you). Were you present on Tuesday night? Did you see the baby plane that hovered over the Mosque?" Brother Ishmael was stunned, but was overcome by adrenaline, as he was not prepared to respond to such a question. Still he did respond and say without thinking, "Yes, that was me in the baby plane Sister Minister Melissa". She replied, "Brother I'm not joking and since you came in after being on post, you should be in a more serious mode than that. Furthermore, we don't need any distractions. This topic is very sensitive". Brother couldn't stop to save his reputation. He replied, "But I speak the truth, I always did. I was in that baby plane. I know how they work. Allah (God) is my witness". An officer of the M.G.T. who was sitting in the circle said, "Sister Minster hold on. If this brother doesn't stop I'll have to call his Captain who is upstairs. He'll deal with this". And as soon as she said that the Captain appeared. His name was Brother Captain James. He was a strong captain who was humble, yet was known for his strict manner and concern for defense of the Mosque. "What's going on Sister Lieutenant? What's all the commotion?" asked Captain James. "Brother Captain it's nothing. We were just talking about the Mother Plane," she said as she was trying to give Brother Ishmael a chance to save grace. But Brother Ishmael was on a roll. He wouldn't take heed.

He was like a child. "No sir Brother Captain", Brother Ishmael said, "I was saying that I was in the Baby Plane you all saw on Tuesday night. It was me. Allah (God) is my witness and I was also on the wheel with the Messenger and he spoke to me." At this point everyone in the circle became very angry. "Don't lie on the Messenger", shouted a believer who was in the circle. Another shouted, "Brother Captain tell him to shut his mouth. He's a liar". Another who had never been to the Mosque started to walk away, so an M.G.T. quickly noticed and ran to comfort her and she stood firm. The Captain of the F.O.I. ordered Brother Ishmael into his office. Asst. Minister Melissa struggled, but regained order and the meeting was restored to a peaceful state. She then said to the group, "We will say a special prayer from the heart for our brother in hopes that he will return to Allah." They didn't believe Brother Ishmael. But there was one brother in the group who did. His name was Brother Elijah. He was a new visitor, never seen there before. He said, "I believe him. Why would he lie and put himself on the spot like that. Maybe he did experience something phenomenal that was related to our experience on Tuesday. He might not understand his experience any more than we do." Sister Minster replied, "You could be right brother. However, his outburst was without value and we don't tolerate that here. He could need spiritual help or even a more; clinical analysis." "You mean a psychiatrist," said a young sister who was in the group with them. "Yes, my sister, now let's move on", said the sister Minister. She then added, "He might be chastised for having sinned".

Meanwhile in the Captains office, Brother Ishmael was having a hard time explaining himself. He had no proof of his claim and would not back down. He was ordered by the Captain to return to F.O.I. Class next week. When the day of class came the Investigators told him that he had to be put out for one year (for breaking a restrictive law: No Lying) and in addition bring a note from a doctor who could verify that he was sane and safe to be among other people. Needless to say, he could also return if he could prove his claim 100 percent. They just didn't believe him and Brother Ishmael was in a whole heap of trouble. It wasn't until that very long night when he went home and cried that he remembered the words that his new brother spoke to him before he left the Mother Ship and returned from his out of body experience. Brother Ishmael then started to read the Quran and reflect on the lives of others who had experienced similar things. He realized that he was wrong in speaking of his experience before the people. Sharing such wisdom at the time was out of season. He didn't understand his experience in full for himself yet. Furthermore, to reveal this experience of being on the Great Wheel to those whom were not aware of his divinity was very careless.

Late that night his ears started to ring again. "Brother Ishmael" a voice said within the ringing, "Brother Ishmael", continuing. "You will soon know the meaning of these things, be not tormented over this", said the voice. Brother Ishmael couldn't make out who it was. Although he had a deep feeling that it was Master Fard Muhammad Himself. His ears rang throughout the night and he could not bare it, but his heart was still. He was confident now that his work and his mission were soon to begin.

Brother Ishmael never returned to the Mosque with a doctor's note. Instead he knew that his mission was to help his Nation and people (The Righteous) from a different vantage point. He knew he would one day return to meet with the Messenger, The Most Honorable Elijah

Muhammad on the Wheel (Great Mother Ship) at a later time. What is his mission? Time will tell, but let's just say...

To Be Continued...

SENISTAR ™

Introduction

This tale takes place in Far Rockaway Queens, New York City. It's a story which I wrote on September 19, 2007. It like the others was originally a bed time story and I just loved telling it so much that I had to add it to this book and make a revision. How my child reacted? Well, if you tell the story correctly by changing your voice (to fit the characters), and making timed gestures being very animated as I instructed when you tell the story to children, you'll then see how my child reacted though the reactions of your own.

This story is dear to me. I like many of you experienced strange or phenomenal occurrences, which till this day go unexplained fully. If we all reached back into our past we would probably find an occurrence or two in our history which mirrors in similarity the greatness of Brother Freedman's experience in this tale. That's how I knew Allah (God) was always there in my life. Also, remember these Baby Planes are real and exist, I have seen many of them right here in New York City.

Have fun reading it. Peace!

The Boy with the Spaced Out Pencil

It was the night before the 1st day of school in Far
Rockaway, New York City. Here in this town lived a
young boy by the name of Brother Freedman. He was only
7 years old and on his way to the 2nd Grade. He was a very
good child, amazingly studious and helpful to his mother.
All the children loved him and he loved good people. He
wasn't afraid of anything either, his mother taught him to
be wise and fearless. However, there are some things that
no matter how much you teach a child, they will naturally
fear. The unimaginable happened to this wonderful child.
He had a close encounter of the most bizarre kind. This
was one for the record books at his school, PS 105 which
was located on Beach 50th Street. It was only a few blocks
from Brother Freedman's house.

Brother Freedman lived alone as an only child with his
mother Clara in a single family house. This neighborhood
was "out of site". It was bordered at its sides by water and
sat within a peninsula, the ocean on one side and the bay on
the other. Brother Freedman could see John F. Kennedy
Air Port from his bedroom window. On this night before
the 1st day of school he was at the window immediately
after dinner. He loved to see the planes roar in for landings
and take off towards the sky at night. He loved it because
at night the runway, and tower lights were on and it looked
like a party to him. To add a little spice, Brother
Freedman would turn on his little CD player and rock
(play) his cartoon music. He would listen to all his
favorites while watching the planes do their thing. Up
planes would go, and down planes would go, and there
would brother Freedman be in his room singing. He soon
would get tired and his mother surely would know because
when all the singing would stop that's when Brother

Freedman's eyes would close. They would flutter and he would nod, then he'd rub his eyes and rock. "Knock, Knock", his mother would be at his door, and then she would say, "It's time for bed". She entered in room with a bag. Brother Freedman was happy to see that his mother brought a surprise. It was a new book bag for him to take to school. "Now here's your new book bag my son, and I want you to take good care of it", said his mother. "Okay mommy", Brother Freedman replied. She gave him the bag as they sat on his bed. He opened it and to his surprise, there were many colorful pencils, books, crayons, pencil sharpeners, and more than he would need. So together they sorted things out and made it lighter for him to carry. He hugged his mom, and kissed her cheek like all good boys would do. They prayed together and asked for guidance from the Lord. They had a great day, but the night was still young. "Did you brush your teeth?" asked his mother. "Yes mommy, I did, I always do before I watch the planes remember", he replied. "Yes, I remember that's what you told me but I am mommy and mommy still has to check", she explained to him with a great big smile. "I love you mommy", he said while looking towards the window. Suddenly a great flash of light illuminated the room from outside. Brother Freedman saw an object which he couldn't describe pass by. "Did you see that mommy", he said. "Oh no, but the room sure did get bright all of the sudden", she replied. "It was a weird light, like a plane's light", he said. Then he ran towards the window and shouted, "Come back, come back". And this was the beginning of his greatest encounter.

The light never returned, and it was getting late so Brother Freedman's mom kissed him good night and tucked him in to bed. Brother Freedman fell fast asleep. She then went to the kitchen to clean up a bit and she noticed as she entered the kitchen that it was already clean. She couldn't remember cleaning it. She pondered for a while till she gave up wondering. Then she went to bed. Before she could close her eyes, the light returned. Her bedroom glowed and her window revealed the presence of a mighty plane. "Oh my God", she shouted and she walked slowly to her window. But as soon as she got there it flew away. She did get a glimpse but that's it. She was in shock, for she never experienced seeing anything like this. She quickly grabbed a drawing pad, and started to draw an image of what she saw. She then picked up the phone and called her brother Leonard who was a registered member of the Nation of Islam. He had been trying to convince his sister to come to a Meeting to learn of the great teachings of the Honorable Elijah Muhammad. So she dialed his number and he picked up the phone. "Peace! Sister, how are you. What's wrong?" he answered as his pitch went from high to low as he sensed her fear. Franticly she bolted, "Brother, I saw it, it was blue, red, white and bright as a Christmas tree". "Okay sister, calm down, for one, you know I don't like to hear about Christmas Trees, remember the Bible, Jeremiah 10 speaks against that!", he said with a stern reply. "Oh, brother it's not that, believe me, I saw a baby plane (a so-called U.F.O.) as you described, it didn't dawn on me until I drew it on paper", she stated. The conversation went on throughout the night, and little did she know that while she was talking to her brother that very same craft was on the other side of the house and near her son's window.

The book bag that Brother Freedman's mother gave him was left open and by his bed. The window where Brother Freedman watched was also wide open. The Baby Plane's pilot was on a mission by the command of the Christ which was to prepare the young child (Brother Freedman) with an experience that he would never forget or be able to explain until an appropriate time. The pilot was a master of telepathy and an artist. He could move objects from far distances without touching them. And he used his gifts to create a pencil that would appear to have extraordinary powers. Out from the Baby Plane flew a pencil that was colored in the brightest and unusual markings; it was also distinguishable by its thickness and infrequent illuminations. By using his power of telepathy the pilot caused this pencil to float from the Baby Plane through the boy's window, and into his new book bag. Mean while back at Brother Freedman's mother's room the phone conversation was getting very deep into the sciences of life, and beyond. The information that his Uncle was sharing was intense, yet soothing. "Thanks so much for explaining this to me, I never thought that angels could be original people and I'm thankful to Allah (God) to have you as a brother", she said while tears of joy rolled from her eyes. She was happy as the reality blossomed, she had witnessed a miracle. "It's my duty as your brother, to share with you what I have for myself, I love you sister and have a good night and don't you worry", he assured her. "Oh, I'm alright, good night brother", she replied. "Don't forget to buy that book, Message to the Black Man tomorrow", he reminded. "Oh I won't, toodle-loo", she gestured and they both hung up.

She was very tired but like always, she would check on her son before she went to bed. As she approached his room she noticed that same light which was quite distinctive from any light she ever saw like the baby plane it came from. She then ran towards the door of Brother Freedman's room and the light went away as soon as she touched the door knob. She opened the door quickly but there was nothing new there. Her child Freedman was just as she left him, cuddled and resting like he was in heaven. He even had a slight smile on his face as if he was having a good dream. This made her feel better but like a good mother she got right beside him and fell fast asleep. No way was she going to let her baby sleep alone, not on this night. And she having experienced such a phenomenon didn't quite feel like sleeping alone either.

The next morning she awoke, and they were late. Her alarm clock was in her bedroom. She looked at the clock on her son's wall and it read 9 am. School starts at 9:30 am. What was she going to do? "Freedman get up, we're late". "How come Mommy?" he replied while his eyes were still closed. "Freedman get up, never mind how come, just get up", she answered. So they both rushed and brushed their teeth in the bathroom. They washed their faces, and got all their things together and dressed quickly. "Mommy we forgot to pray", said Brother Freedman. "Okay, let's pray while we walk", she stated with a smile. "While we walk, that's crazy mommy!" he said while chuckling. "No it's not, we can talk to the Father just like you're talking to your mother while you're walking", she wisely explained. And so while walking out the house with all their things, the book bag and all they needed they prayed a short and powerful prayer. "Oh God, please protect us and continue to guide us, as we thank you for all that you gave us, Amen". The walk wasn't far, but there was still the problem, Brother Freedman was going to be late for his 1st day of school and this didn't resound well in Clara's mind at all She always taught her son to be on time for school. Brother Freedman could sense as they were walking that his mother was sad over the lateness. He said lovingly, "Mommy don't you worry, it wasn't your fault that we were late, we had a bizarre night, not everyone had a night like ours". "Oh baby boy, you're my hero, you've made Mommy feel so much better, and you're right we did have a weird yet holly night." She confirmed, then with greater confidence they walked to school.

When they got to the doors of P.S. 105 classes had already been assigned to the students. Brother Freedman's mother took her son to the main office. There she met with the principal and explained that her son was late. The principal arranged for Brother Freedman and his mother to be directed to his home class room and so they both went together to meet with the teacher whose name was Ms. Dance-child. Needless to say, after hearing what the teachers name was they both looked at each other with that look that says, "If we were alone we'd be cracking up a fool (laughing hard)". They held in their laughter and walked to the class to meet her. The class was already situated and students were asking questions when they knocked on the door. Ms. Dance-child came to answer. She was tall, African and beautiful. She had a smile on her that could light up minds of decadence. "Good morning and who might you be?" she asked. "I'm Clara, and this is my son Freedman, it's good to meet you Ms. Dance-child. Sorry he's late, but I really have to go to work, I'll talk to you later as I really don't want to disturb you any further", Brother Freedman's mother replied. "Oh, I know, and don't worry we all have our bad days, but remember all things happen for good reasons even when we don't know why. Have a nice day Clara. I'll take good care of your son", said Ms. Dance-child. Clara just smiled, and as she walked away, Ms. Dance-Child hugged Brother Freedman and said, "Hi, you can sit in the back; all the seats in the front are taken". "Oh, I don't want to sit in the back, I like the front", he said in sorrow. "Don't worry Freedman, now go on and sit in that fine seat, and pay close attention", she said. Brother Freedman obeyed and sat way in the back, but he wasn't the only one there, this class was packed with about 20 students. It was quite orderly though; all the children were well behaved.

"Okay class simmer down, we have a new student. Everyone say Good morning to Freedman", said Ms. Dance-child. "GOOD MORINNG FREEDMAN", shouted all the children with glee. "Now that you all know each other please take out your pencils and note books, we're going to do a check on your supplies to see if you all have what you're supposed to, and those who do not have what they're supposed to we're going to help you with that", added Ms. Dance-child.

Brother Freedman went into his note book and couldn't find a pencil, and he went in all the pockets of his note book too. He searched and searched until his teacher stopped him from searching. "Freedman is something wrong", she asked. "I can't find my pencil, and we had a lot of them last night in my bag", he replied. "Did you check the front pocket of your book bag", she suggested. "Oh, I forgot I'm sorry", he said. He checked the front pocket and pulled out a regular No.2 pencil. "Okay class now I would like you to take your pencils and write your names down along with your headings just as you see on the black board", she said to the class as she referred to an example of the proper heading which she demonstrated on the black board. Most of the children were successful at writing the heading in their notebooks while Brother Freedman's pencil broke at the tip. "Ms. Dance-child, Ms. Dance-Child", shouted Brother Freedman. "Yes, Freedman what's wrong this time", she replied. "My pencil broke, it's not working", he said. "Did you try to see if you have another in the front pocket of your book bag little one?" asked Ms. Dance-child. "Oh, I'm sorry I didn't check like that", answered Brother Freedman. So he then went into his bag and saw that big colorful pencil that was placed in the bag by the pilot of the Baby Plane while he slept last night. Brother Freedman was quite shocked, he didn't see this pencil before, and he as so amazed at the rich colors and strange writings on the pencil, and they were actually Arabic a language he did not know. He knew that if he used this pencil that it would draw attention but he didn't have another one. "Oh well, this must have been in there last night from Mommy", he said to himself. So he started to write his name and heading when suddenly the pencil popped out of his hand and fell on the floor in an instant all by itself. "Ahhh", shouted brother Freedman, and he jumped onto the floor to find his pencil. All the children in the back of the class laughed at him as he scrambled to pick it up. "Freedman, what's wrong with you today, you're distracting the class, now get your act together", shouted Ms. Dance-child. Brother Freedman retrieved the odd pencil and tried to complete his heading. It was no use, the pencil popped out of his hand and floated back into the front pocket of his book bag which he left open. "Ahhh", he shouted, as he scrambled once again to find his pencil. He darted into his book bag. "Now class stay focused on your work", said Mr. Dance-child, as she made her way slowly towards Brother Freedman. The sound from the heels of her shoes echoed as it were a countdown to Armageddon. "Ooooh, you're in trouble", said one of the children. Brother Freedman was still scrambling to find his pencil. Ms. Dance-child said as she closed in on him, "Freedman, I met your mother and she doesn't seem like the type that I see in you at this time, what are you doing?" "I'm sorry my pencil keeps popping out of my hand, it's not my fault", said the innocent Freedman. The teacher shouted, "Pencils don't just pop out of hands, hold on to it, and if you continue to disrupt my class I'll have to send you to the Dean's Office for detention. I do not tolerate class clowns". "I'm no clown", replied Brother Freedman. "We shall see, now finish your heading", said Ms. Dance-child giving him the benefit of the doubt as she calmed down a bit. As the teacher walked back to the front Brother Freedman while other students were watching grabbed the pencil out of his bag and said in a soft yet commanding tone, "Now you stop it magic pencil, stop it and stay in my hand". The children who witnessed him talking to the pencil started to converse and giggle at the troubled Freedman. Luckily the commotion didn't bother Ms. Dance-child much though she did notice she flicked it off her mind like a light switch. She had too much work to do. Here experience would not allow her to lose focus.

Brother Freedman gained control again and started to finish his heading on the page at his desk again. Then the colorful pencil started to glow with lights. Then it cut off just like a flash. "Ahhh", screamed brother Freedman and he dropped the pencil onto the floor. "Now that's it young man, you've got some explaining to do right now", shouted Ms. Dance-child to Brother Freedman who didn't see any of that. "It's my pencil Ms. Dance-child, its crazy", he insisted. All the children started laughing very loudly. It was becoming a scene to remember when Ms. Dance-child laid down the law and said, "This is what happens to class clowns, you go to the Dean's office, now get, it's on the main floor near the main office. Come get your hall pass Freedman right now", she ordered. While she was ordering him the pencil popped into his book bag without anyone noticing. Brother Freedman wanted to find his pencil to put it in his bag. Ms. Dance-child scolded him, "you're acting like a little squander of a boy and this is not proper at all, I will also write a letter to your mother". The poor boy was looking for his pencil, he couldn't find it and so he just took his bag and went to the front of the class room to Ms. Dance-child and said, "I'm sorry Ms. Dance-child" in a soft sincere manner. He then took the hall pass from her extended hand and went on his way out the door to the Dean's office.

While on his way to the Dean's and in the hall outside of the class he bumped into a Hall Monitor who was a bit older than him and in the 5th Grade. His name was Brother Jerry who asked, "What are you doing in the hallway?" Brother Freedman replied, "I'm on my way to the Dean's Office" while showing Brother Jerry the Hall Pass. Little did he know the front pocket of his book bag was left open. The pencil popped out and hit Brother Jerry in the back of his head while they were walking then it fell on the floor. Then Brother Freedman shouted, "Ahhh" but it was too late. Brother Jerry was furious! "You hit me with that crazy looking pencil in my head", he said. "No I didn't, that pencil has a mind of its own, I was looking for it", shouted Brother Freedman. "Who are you yelling at", Brother Jerry demanded? The two boys began to shout angrily at each other when another Teacher named Ms. Friday approached them during their shouting match. Ms. Friday said, "Boys, both of you are coming with me to the Dean's Office now, be quite and come with me right now". Now going to the Dean's office was like going to jail in school, it spelled detention, suspension, and if you did badly enough as a child a beating at home by your parents. This was not the place to be. "Ms. Friday let me explain", said Brother Jerry. "I don't want to hear it, you tell it to the Dean, be quite, I don't want to hear another word", she said, and she meant business. They quietly both walked quietly with her to the main floor. Now Brother Freedman didn't even pick up the pencil, but it found its way back into his bag again floating with ease and unnoticed right behind them as they walked to the Dean's Office.

The Dean wasn't very patient and very stern. His name was Mr. Don-Dada. He used to be a nicer individual and really cool, but ever since the government outlawed smoking in public places he became like a tyrant. Mr. Don-Dada is a chain smoker of cigarettes and even cigars. He doesn't care much about the rising death tolls of those who smoked. Every day he grunts about the law that keeps him from smoking in the school. In many ways he's a bit crazy. He even had an uncle who died of cancer caused by smoking and still won't stop himself. The children are terrified of him, but because he adheres to the law and doesn't get too crazy he's manages to keep his job. Many of the teachers like him but pray every day that he recognizes that smoking is not good for him and that one day he'll stop and return to his cool self. They say he was like a prophet in his own right, calm and collective, but not nowadays.

Ms. Friday busted into the office with both boys in her hands, "Dean Don-Dada, take these two off my hands I have work to do". Then she stormed out and left the two boys to fend from themselves against the grunting Dean. Dean Don-Dada spoke, "Both of you sit right in the seats before you, I'm on the phone so be quiet!!!" Then the boys sat down but they didn't listen to well. "Where's that pencil you hit me with", asked Brother Jerry of Brother Freedman. "I don't have it, I left it in the hallway", replied Brother Freedman (he didn't know that the pen was in his bag). "You have it, I'm going to find it", said Brother Jerry and he grabbed his bag. That's when they started to tug over the bag. "Give me, my bag", demanded brother Freedman as he pulled it back from Brother Jerry. Dean

Don-Dada while on the phone said to his friend whom he was speaking to "I have to call you back duty calls" and then he hung up the phone. He began rolling up his sleeves and Brother Jerry noticed. "BOYS", shouted Dean Don-Dada. They both stood up at attention and started to give excuses. "He grabbed my bag", shouted Brother Freedman. "He hit me with a pencil in the Hallway", shouted Brother Jerry. "WHAT BOTH OF YOU SIT DOWN DON'T LET ME HAVE TO CALL YOUR MOTHERS IN", shouted Dean Don-Dada. They didn't want that so they immediate sat down quietly. "Now what's your name?" asked Dean Don-Dada as he pointed to Brother Freedman. "My name is Freedman, Brother Freedman", he replied. "Well Brother Freedman, is it true, did you hit him with a pencil in the hallway", asked Dean Don-Dada? "Not exactly", replied Brother Freedman. "What do you mean, not exactly, where is the pencil", asked Dean Don-Dada? And just as the Dean asked the pencil poked out of the front pocket of Brother Freedman's bag (it was like a nightmare). Brother Freedman said, "I think I left it in the hallway". Then Dean Don-Dada saw the pencil sticking out of his bag and asked, "What in the world kind of pencil is that, is that the pencil?" The boys looked down at the bag and that's when Brother Jerry started to shout. "See I told you, I knew you had it", he shouted. "QUIET", ordered Dean Don-Dada. "Didn't I tell you to be quiet", he added? "But Dean Don-Dada, this boy is a liar; he told me that he didn't have the pencil", cried Brother Jerry. Poor Brother Freedman, he had no idea that he was that this event was going to change his life forever. Who would have thought that all this time he was being prepared for a greater cause which he would understand in the near future, but he had to go through this pain. He was telling the truth but he had no way of proving it so he began to cry. While sobbing he said, "I know you don't believe me. I didn't lie. I told the truth and this pencil is doing what it wants to do. I can't stop it and I didn't hit you with it". Dean Don-Dada said, "Let me have a look at this pencil" and took it out of Brother Freedman's bag. "Hum, this pencil has Arabic writing on it, and these colors are so beautiful. Where did you get it from", asked the Dean? "I don't know, my mother got if for me ask her", replied Brother Freedman. "Do you want me to call her", asked Dean Don-Dada in a joking manner? "Yeah, call his mother", Brother Jerry taunted. "No, don't call her", said Brother Freedman who was still sobbing.   The mean Dean started to laugh and just as he began to chuckle the pencil popped out of his hand and popped him in the head "BING". "OUCH, WHAT IN THE WORLD", he shouted like Mr. Crabs? Brother Jerry's mouth popped wide open in surprise and brother Freedman stopped sobbing and started to laugh while saying, "See, See, See, See". The pencil began to light up and it rolled under the Deans desk as he grunted, "You better have an explanation for this Brother Freedman." "Ha, Ha, Ha" laughed Brother Freedman. Dean Don-Dada was very angry with Brother Freedman he ordered him to sit down, while he tried to find the pencil that rolled under his desk.   When Dean Don-Dada knelled down he hit his head hard on the edge of his desk "BANG" and the boys both started to laugh, "Ouch" he said again. And while he was on the floor and Brother Jerry was laughing with him, Brother Freedman noticed the Baby Plane appear right outside the window of the Dean's office. He stopped laughing, but the others didn't notice. When Dean Don-Dada recovered he gave up looking for the pencil and said, "I'm going to have to separate the two of you.   Brother Jerry, come with me outside." And he grabbed Brother Jerry by the arm and stood with him outside the door leaving Brother Freedman inside alone. As they were talking the pencil rolled right back from under the desk and stood upright and started to glow. Meanwhile the Baby Plane was moving closer to the building. Brother Freedman could see the Pilot in the window who was waving at Brother Freedman. All of the sudden the pencil floated upwards and levitated right in front of Brother Freedman. Meanwhile as he stood and watched, outside the office Dean Don-Dada as he was finished scolding Brother Jerry and told him to return to his duties. "I'll take care of Brother Freedman don't you worry now get back you monitoring the halls", said Dean Don-Dada. He had no idea what he was about to witness and his mind was about to change as he made it up to punish Brother Freedman for supposedly lying as he presumed. Dean Don-Dada opened his door and to his surprise he watched as the pencil lit up and floated right past his face and out of his window. Brother Freedman's eyes were wide open like light bulbs and the Dean started to mumble, "Da, da, da, da, da," "Is that why they call you Don –Dada", asked Brother Freedman in a joking manor? They both walked to the window to where the pencil floated. The Baby Plane then took off in the sky as they both watched. "Don't you tell, and I won't tell", suggested Dean Freedman who like Brother Freedman had never seen anything like a Baby Plane before. "I won't tell anyone but I want a Lollypop", said Brother Freedman. "Here, take the whole bag. You can't go wrong now, that pencil is gone up with whatever that was. You head back to your class and tell your teacher that I spoke to you", said Dean Don-Dada while handing him a large bag of Lollypops. This was the day that Brother Freedman and Dean Don-Dada became the best of friends. It was through this experience that they bonded, and would never tell a soul of what happened. "I'm going to stop smoking today", said Dean Don-Dada. "Yeah, Yeah", shouted Brother Freedman and he took his bag of candy and his book bag and dashed down the hall shouting, "Dean Don –Dada, stopped smoking, Dean Don-Dada stopped smoking", as class room doors opened and teachers popped their heads out of them. While Brother Freedman was on his way upstairs Dean Don-Dada called his teacher from his office. He called to tell her that she didn't have to worry about him, and also she didn't have to write a report to his mother.

While on the way home from School Brother Freedman told his mother the entire story. They laughed way into the night about it. And at about 7 o'clock the door bell rang. It was Uncle Leonard. Sister Clara answered the door and to her surprise there he was with a bag of gifts in his hand. "Oh Leonard my good brother what a surprise", she said while giving him a great big hug. Brother Freedman dashed into them and nearly knocked them down. He was so happy to see him. "Uncle Leonard, Uncle Leonard, you won't believe what happened today", he said. "I brought you two some gifts", said Uncle Leonard. "What you got there", asked Mother Clara? "It's the book that I just know you forgot to buy today, remember *Message to the Black Man*. And for you my little nephew it's an air plane", said Uncle Leonard with a jolly old spirit. Brother Freedman ran into his room with his brand new red and white air plane. "Hey I thought you had to tell me something?" asked Uncle Leonard. "Oh, don't worry I'll tell him, you just go on and play son", said Mother Clara. "You wouldn't believe what happened today, and on top of that, you wouldn't believe what his teachers name is, ha, ha", started Mother Clara.

To be continued?

The Break Down

SENISTAR ™

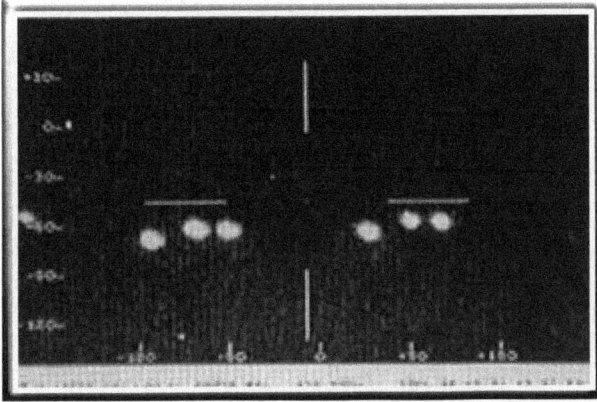

This photo is of actual Baby Planes taken by the
Mexican Air Force during a routine flight on May 3,
1994. More than 1 dozen were filmed in their area of
flight. You can see a good portion of this video at
www.Godswater7.com or www.Mosque7.org

SENISTAR ™

The Truth of the so called UFO

Holy Quran 24:43
Seest though not that Allah drives along the clouds, then gathers them together, then piles them up, so that thou seest the rain coming forth from their midst? And He sends down from the heaven (clouds like) mountains, wherein is hail, afflicting therewith whom He pleases and turning it away from whom He pleases. The Flash of His lighting almost takes away the sight. Allah causes the night and the day to succeed one another. Surely there is a lesson in this for those who have sight."

Brothers and sisters (The Righteous),

Peace,

I really couldn't end this book without giving you some actual facts concerning these phenomenal planes. Many are witnessing them today in major cities throughout the world. Before I do I have been guided to inform you of a great sign that is present which all of you can see from your homes.

A Discovery and Great Sign of the Arrival

Holy Quran 10:6 *"Surely in the variation of the night and the day, and that which Allah has created in the heavens and the earth, there are signs for a people who keep their duty."*

Why a sign? According to the scriptures which were revealed to Prophets by Allah (God) there will be signs in both the heavens and earth of the coming of Allah (God) in the flesh. The Son of Man, a man who has been given command over all things. He comes at the end of the time of evil (Satan), which was given a 6000 year period of rule over the earth and all its inhabitants (ref. *A Message to the Blackman*). The Son of Man comes to destroy.

According to what we have all been taught (in schools across America) with regards to the moon it has 2 sides, one that is illuminated by the sunlight and the other dark. The Honorable Elijah Muhammad teaches that the moon boroughs it's light from the sun. This makes sense for the moon is as a dry rock and is referred to by Allah (God) as a dry olive branch. It cannot generate its own light. It's mysterious to most. I wish to at a point in time share some information on the truth as taught by Elijah of its origin if it pleases Allah (God)?

Getting back to the sign; the moon has several stages, during its journey around the planet Asia (earth) which is rotating at the terrific speed of 1,037 1/3 miles per hour on its own axis. Our moon has a great love for the planet earth. Like a magnet it pulls on the earth's waters. The earth is the mother of the moon, as the Honorable Elijah Muhammad has taught. This moon's stages are from crescent to full.

The rationalization for one of the magnificent displays of relationships between heavens planets and stars from the scientist of this world has become widely incomplete. This is my humble opinion of course. Allow me to explain what Allah (God) has allowed me to see for you.

Allah (God) has come, there's no use to sing and wait for Him. He's already here. Surely this is profound, but let this great sign that He has allowed me to see stand. I am so honored by His grace to have the opportunity to share this with you. Have no illusions, The Son of Man, whom I believe to be Master Fard Muhammad is in complete control of the universe!

Have you noticed how the moon has behaved lately? It's brighter than ever and sometimes looks so close to the earth, it almost looks as if it could land on the planet. Scientist of this world taught us that the moon's stages are produced by the Sun which shines its light on it, while the earth is between the sun and the moon. The union causes a shadow like effect which is seen on the moon's surface from earth. If the sun is directly behind the moon we get what is called, a Solar Eclipse. If the earth is between the moon and the sun and we look at it we can see something like this at night (Figure 1).

Figure 1: the moon at night, during the 2nd stage.

This makes some sense. We're (on earth) between the sun and the moon, so the moon is in our shadow, the earth's shadow. It's possible, but now I wonder if it's absolutely necessary for our planet to be between the two (sun and moon) for this effect to take place. Is the moon truly in our shadow all the time during this? In fact I really doubt it now. Light travels around the first of two adjacent objects after long distances are made between them. Lift your hand from the ground on a sunny day; you'll see what I mean. Watch your hands shadow disappear after about 1-2 feet. Then re-consider the distances between the sun, earth and the moon. The distance between the earth and the sun is 93 Million Miles (ref. Honorable Elijah Muhammad). And according to NASA scientist the distance between the earth and moon's centers are about 385,000 miles (ref. LPI Bulletin, No. 72, August, 1994, Nasa.gov). The diameter of the sun is 853,000 miles and the earth's is 7,926 miles (ref. Honorable Elijah Muhammad). The diameter of the moon is approximately 3,476 miles (ref. Exploring the Moon, NASA EG-1997-10-116-HQ). You scientist in government will be forced to re-examine. My gut feeling is that something is not right of what the scholars of this world have taught us with regards to space and light! The Messenger of Allah (God) was 100 percent right and exact! Think over this.

Sometime during the 1994 I noticed that the moon was in crescent shape during the day time at around 11 a.m. It was in a period of my life when Allah (God) was really coming to light within me as I grew in understanding of Him. This occurrence was most unusual, but I was so elated because it didn't take me long to believe in what I was seeing. I couldn't keep from looking at it. I had to bare witness. The moon wasn't itself. Now you might say this is nothing, but what was even more astonishing was the fact that the Sun was right next to it in its orbit. There I was looking at these two great works of Allah (God) and there was nothing between them but time, and space yet the moon appeared to evade my eye partially. What normally would have been a dark side during its 2nd or 3rd stages was totally gone from sight. The moon was fading away. Allow me to explain. When the moon is in its crescent stage during the night it shows the illuminated side and the dark side is merged with the darkness of space. However during the day, I saw that (dark) side but it was not visible at all, and while the sun was right next to it above the earth.

This picture paints an idea of what I experienced exactly. Pay attention to the shape of the moon as it orbits near the sun. Ref. Figure 2

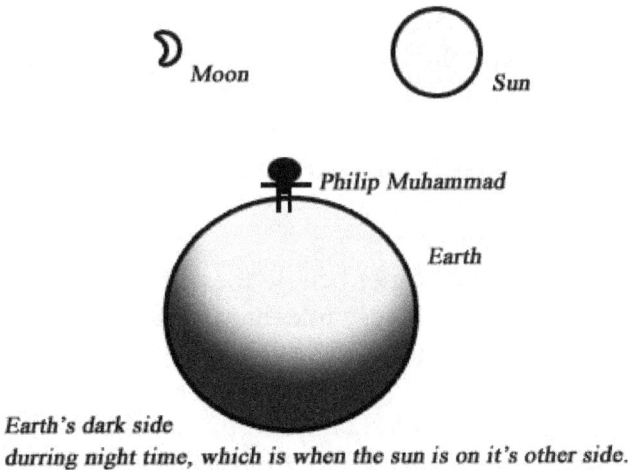

Figure 2: the sun, moon, and earth at approximately 11 a.m. EST.

How could it be? The sun facing the moon's left side should produce a full moon. But in this case (and you can all see it for yourself in time) the sun doesn't produce all sides of the moon with its light. The sun's rays of light have a range of over 76 quintillion miles. Its energy keeps all the planets rotating at the same speed of 1037 1/3 miles per hour (ref: Theology of Time, Audio). If its energy is constant then so should be its light, no? Furthermore, and again, there was nothing between the sun and the moon to help to produce this effect. But of course there could not be a shadow in this case. What was preventing me from seeing the side of the moon which disappeared right in my eye view? It remained like that all day, even at dawn. You can all look and see this for yourself (at the appropriate time). I don't believe this is going away. You all can see it, just give it a few days, wait till you see the moon during the day. I'm sorry that I can't tell you exactly when.

There is a purpose for it (this great sign), and it is as I have said, the Lord Has Come, and I saw this years ago back in 1994. As it continues to manifest, the moon appears to be folded up. I wonder if the sun is next. This is clear evidence of The Superior Being at work, not a plain discovery at all! A universal change is apparently taking place that dispels this worlds understanding of just what takes place in the heavens.

Before we go any further behold these excerpts from scripture; they are all very relevant in many more ways than the most obvious:

Holy Quran: Surah 81:2 "When the sun is folded up, and when the stars are dust coloured, And when the mountains are made to pass away, And when the camels are abandoned, And when the wild animals are gathered together, and when the cities are made to swell, And when the men are united... " *(By the way, this chapter of the Quran is called "The Folding Up".*

Holy Quran: Surah 22:23 "Surely Allah will make those who believe and do good deeds enter Gardens wherein flow rivers – they are adorned therein with bracelets of gold and with pearls. And their garments therein are of silk, and they are guided to pure words, and they are guided on the path of the Praised One. Those who disbelieve and hinder (men) from Allah's way and from the Sacred Mosque, which We have made equally for all men, (for) the dweller therein and the visitor. And whoever inclines therein to wrong, unjustly, We shall make him taste of painful chastisement."

Holy Quran: Surah 86:9 "On the day when hidden things are manifested, Then he will have no strength, nor helper. By the cloud giving rain…"

Holy Quran: Surah 91:1 "By the sun and his brightness! And the moon when she borrows light from him! And the day when it exposes it to view!" (Could this one parable hold the clue to the cause of the effect I am pointing out? The borrowed light of the moon is what we are seeing as the moon is in orbit over us during the day. But what's blocking the part we cannot see?)

There are worshipers of the sun whom under the influence may worship the moon as it has learned to evade the suns light. But it neither the moon nor sun have power of its own creation so what are they (the sun worshipers) going to do? What they and other polytheist should do is turn towards the Creator who has power over all things. Atheist (who don't believe in God) surely have no reason to doubt that a great force is truly showing forth power in this case with the power to make a portion of the moon **disappear** in real-time and space, or appear to.

Some marvel over Hollywood magicians on earth who use trickery. Even those magicians who have been granted some extraordinary abilities by Allah (God) have to turn towards the light of the Son of Man (Master of The Day of Judgment).

Holy Quran: Surah 27:13 (of the days of Moses) "So when Our clear signs came to them, they said: This is clear enchantment. And they denied them unjustly and proudly, while their souls were convinced of them. See them, what was the end of the mischief makers! And certainly we gave knowledge to David and Solomon. And they said; Praises be to Allah, Who has made us excel many of His believing servants!"

Remember, life is not to be taken and from the beginning we borough our souls under a contract written in our blood.

Everyone Will See Them
As a brother of the righteous, I have to encourage you to study deeply into spirits and rise above your emotions and into the thinking of God (as taught by Minister Louis Farrakhan). You should have a great yearning to know exactly who you are as you relate to scripture. You must know yourself for only then will you know your Lord, the true Master of the Day of Requital. In the later pages of this book you will find book references which I strongly advise you to read. Reading a book once doesn't insure your understanding of what the writer or presenter is offering to share with you. As you grow and re-read the literature again and again you will find deeper understanding, having found faith.

Within the book, "Message to the Blackman in America" and audio tape compilation "The Theology of Time", by the Honorable Elijah Muhammad he makes reference to these terrific crafts of flight we all know as UFO's. However as I have mentioned before, these are not "unidentified flying objects". They have been identified. Even in the book of Ezekiel you will find them to be known as "Cherubs" of Jehovah (Bible, 10th Chapter of Ezekiel). Elijah explains in depth the origin of them, and of how the largest of them was built (to the date of the writing) and other details that are beyond fascinating. I'll share some details with you now.

Bible: Ezekiel
1:8 "And there were the hands of man under their wings on their four sides…"
1:12 "And they would go each one straight forward. To wherever the spirit would incline to go, they would go. They would not turn as they went."
1:16 "As for the appearance of the wheels and their structure, it was like the glow of chryso-lite, and the four of them had one likeness. And their appearance and their structure were just as when a wheel proved to be in the midst of a wheel."

There were 1500 hundred of them at the time Elijah was taught of them by his teacher, Master Fard Muhammad. And each one of them had 3 bombs of 100 percent dynamite with drills on them that enable them to travel deeply through the earth. Once the bomb reaches its point of destination it ignites sending earth in the opposite direction and about causing a mountain to erect equal in size to the length of its travel from point A (the surface of the earth) to point B (it's destination). These craft are called by Allah (God), "Baby Planes" (in English). They are the smaller ones that most people who have sighted the now **IFO's (Identified Flying Objects)** have seen.

One would be wise to ask, "Shouldn't we be afraid of them?" "Well of coarse", I'd say. We should fear none but the Master of the Day of Judgment. He drives in these planes along with His Christ (who has been granted command), and the angels. And some of you thought that today's "smart bombs" were new to the original man, not so, there's nothing new under our sun.

There is a greater plane that was mentioned by the Honorable Elijah Muhammad. The Mother Ship, it's terrifyingly huge at one-half mile by a half mile in diameter. It is also known as "the Great Wheel". This great plane along with the smaller ones can travel at speeds beyond our eyes ability to track, and cut and turn in an instant even at hair pin degrees without destructing. I heard a scientist in a video on Google Video say that these wheels are made lighter during flight in order to beat the laws of gravity.

The Honorable Elijah Muhammad taught us that on it is a farm, and people just like you and I (original people). There are differences in that these people operate as would true, progeny (off spring) of the Most High God!

This Mother Ship is capable of destroying each country on the entire planet. But don't worry. He (the Son of Man) does want to rid the earth of all the evil people, and every sign of their having ever existed.

Recently in the month of February of 2006 NASA (the National Aeronautics and Space Administration) recorded an incident where an energy harnessing conductor cable called a Tether was mysteriously dethatched from its space station Columbia during and exercise by way of an overload of power as it orbited over Northern Africa. The Tether was designed to collect electrons from space, 0 point energy. This Tether was also designed to harness the energy to propel shuttles, and even space stations into deeper regions of space. If successful it would save NASA billions in rocket fuel cost per year. It was about 12 miles long and as it drifted away from Columbia dozens of these so-called unidentified objects (Baby Planes) began to surround it. It's safe to say that this incident may have orchestrated by the angles who pilot the baby planes by the permission of the Son of Man.

During the initial recording of the incident NASA representatives are referring to these craft as "Debris" though it's clear by their size and actions that they are more than just debris. I saw a scientist in a video seen online who made an independent analysis. He said that some of these craft according to his findings were over 2 ½ miles in diameter. His explanation was quite sound in my opinion. I would be a fool to think that since the date of the Honorable Elijah Muhammad's book there were not more ships built by our people (the righteous).

I must tell you who are learning of these things for the first time, and who know very little of them, like me, we must simply turn towards the total submission to the will of Allah (God) immediately.

Thank you for reading these words.

Ref: Keyword "Tether Incident" at Google Videos (http://video.google.com) to see recent NASA footage of the Air-Force of the Nation of Islam.

Behold these additional excerpts from scripture;

Holy Quran Surah 46:23 "He said: The knowledge is only with Allah, and I deliver to you that wherewith I am sent, but I see you are an ignorant people. So when they saw it a cloud advancing their valleys, they said: This is a cloud bringing us rain. Nay, it is that which you sought to hasten, a wind where in is painful chastisement. Destroying everything by the command of its Lord. So at dawn naught could be seen except their dwellings. Thus do We reward the guilty people."

Holy Quran Surah 46:27 "And certainly We destroyed the towns round about you, and WE repeat the messages that they may turn..."

Holy Quran Surah 2:62 "Surely those who believe, and those who are Jews, and Christians, and the Sabians, whoever believes in Allah and the Last Day and does good, they have their reward with their Lord, and there is no fear for them, nor shall they grieve."

Call yourself whatever you want, but you had best believe your eyes!

SENISTAR ™

Meet the Author

As-Salaam Alaikum (Peace be unto you),

Thank you for purchasing my first book. I hope that it has become an investment by now, and you and your family have benefited from reading it. I wrote it with the righteous in mind in hopes that you would know that there are people just like you who want a better world for our children.

I would like to thank Allah (God), His Messenger, the Most Honorable Elijah Muhammad, and His Reminder in our midst the Honorable Minister Farrakhan Muhammad. Also I would like to thank a good friend and fellow poet named La'sean Hall-Robinson who helped to inspire me to complete this book. Thanks also goes out to another powerful poet Molika Muhammad of Muhammad Mosque No.7 for taking the time out to help with editing. Surely not least I would like to thank my son for being there always in my corner. Thank you all so very much, and may Allah (God) continue to protect you.

Author: Philip "Senistar" Muhammad

Editor's Choice Award

Presented to

Philip Muhammad

August 2004

For Outstanding Achievement in Poetry

Presented by

poetry.com and the International Library of Poetry

Howard Ely
Managing Editor

The International Library of Poetry
poetry.COM

More Relevant Scripture

Holy Quran

The Disbelievers, Surah 109:1
Say O disbelievers, I server not <u>that which you serve</u>, Nor do you serve <u>Him Whom I serve</u>, not shall I serve <u>that which</u> ye serve not do you serve <u>Him Whom</u> I serve, For you is your recompense and for me is my recompense.

The One Covering Himself Up, Surah 73:14
On the day when the earth and the mountains quake and the mountains become as heaps of sand let loose. Surely We have sent to you a Messenger, a witness against you, as We sent a messenger to Pharaoh.

The Adoration, Surah 32:10
And they say: When we are lost in the earth, shall we then be in a new creation? Nay, they are disbelievers in the meeting with their Lord. Say: The angel of death, <u>who</u> is given charge of you, will cause you to die, then to your Lord you will be returned. (The world would go blind after so-called death of Prophet Muhammad (Peace Be Upon him and all the Messengers) and one would be born to return us to Allah (God).

The Companies, Surah 39:4
If Allah desired to make a son to Himself, He would have chosen those He pleased out of those <u>whom</u> He has created. Glory be to Him – He is Allah The Subduer of All.

Mary Surah, 19:89
Certainly you make an abominable assertion! The heavens may almost rent thereat, and the earth cleave asunder, and

the mountains fall down in pieces, <u>that they ascribe a son</u> to the Beneficent! And it is not worthy of the Beneficent that He should take to Himself a Son.

The Man, Surah 76:17

And round about them are <u>made to go vessels</u> of silver and goblets of glass…

The Man, Surah 76:23

"Surely We have revealed the Quran to thee, in portions. So wait patiently for the judgment of thy Lord, and obey not a sinner or an ungrateful one among therein. And glorify the name of thy Lord morning and evening. And during part of the night adore Him, and glorify Him through-out a long night. Surely these love the transitory life and neglect a grievous day before them. WE created them and made firm their make, and when We will, We can bring in their place the like of them by change. Surely this is a Reminder; so whoever will, let him take a way to his Lord. And you will not, unless Allah please. Surely Allah is ever Knowing Wise. He admits whom He pleases to His mercy; and the wrongdoers – He has prepared for them a painful chastisement."

The Busting Asunder, Surah 84:1

"When the heaven burst asunder, and listens to its Lord and is made fit, and when the earth is stretched, and cast forth what is in it and becomes empty, and listens to its Lord and is made fit, O man, thou must strive a hard striving (to attain) to thy Lord, <u>until thou meet Him.</u> "

Bible

Luke 2:48 (Mary's Words on who is the Father of Jesus)
Now then they saw him they were astounded, and his
mother said to him: Child, why did you treat us this way?
<u>Here your father and I in mental distress have been looking
for you</u>: But he said to them: Why did you have to go
looking for me? Did you not know that I must be in the
house of my Father? However they did not grasp the saying
that he spoke to them."

The words "Mental Distress" are quite clear and they can only be
used to reference the presence of a Physical Man who worried,
or has become weak in faith. In this case it was Joseph (known
as the Carpenter) who was the biological Father of Jesus. The
new and spiritual father Jesus refers to is Lord of The Worlds.
This may have been the first time Jesus revealed it to them.

This means that Mary's (the Mother of Jesus) word goes against
the foundation of every known religion that is based on the so-
called "immaculate conception", I know today is the "immaculate
deception" which in the wake of understanding will experience a
full and truly "immaculate rejection". Tradition can cripple us!

Malachi 1:6
"A son, for his part, honors a father; and a servant, his
grand master. So if I am a father, where is the honor to
me? And if I am a grand master, where is the fear of me?
Jehovah of armies has said to you, O priests who are
despising my name."

Malachi 4:5
"Look! I am sending to YOU people <u>Elijah</u> the prophet
before the coming of the great and fear-inspiring day of
Jehovah. <u>And he must</u> turn the heart of the fathers back
toward sons, and the heart of sons back toward fathers in
order that I may not come and actually strike the earth with
a devoting (of it) to destruction."

SENISTAR ™

Do you still believe in the Immaculate Conception? After you study these scriptures particularly Luke 2:48 and Malachi 1:6 honor Allah (God) and tell your friends, family and the world. And the best way to tell them is to live your life according to the example left to us of the Prophets.

Books to Reference

Author: Allah (God) Who revealed all the scriptures
of the Holy Quran to Prophet Muhammad
(PBUH) 1400 A.D.
Translator: Maulana Muhammad
Book: Holy Quran

Author: Allah (God, The Lord of The Worlds) Who
reveals scripture to all the prophets.
Books: Ezekiel (Chapter 10:2), and Revelations, of
the Bible

Author: The Honorable Elijah Muhammad
Books: "Our Saviour Has Arrived"
"Message to the Blackman in America"
Audio: "The Theology of Time Series"

Author: Jabril Muhammad
Books: "Is It Possible That the Honorable Elijah
Muhammad Is Still Physically Alive"
"Closing the Gap"

For more Senistar visit these sites:
www.Godswater7.com
www.MySpace.com/SenistarNYC

Credits

Author & Graphics: Philip "Senistar" Muhammad
Co-Editors: La'Sean Hall-Robinson
Molika Muhammad
Photography: Malick Fard Muhammad
David Muhammad a.k.a. "Dj"

SENISTAR ™

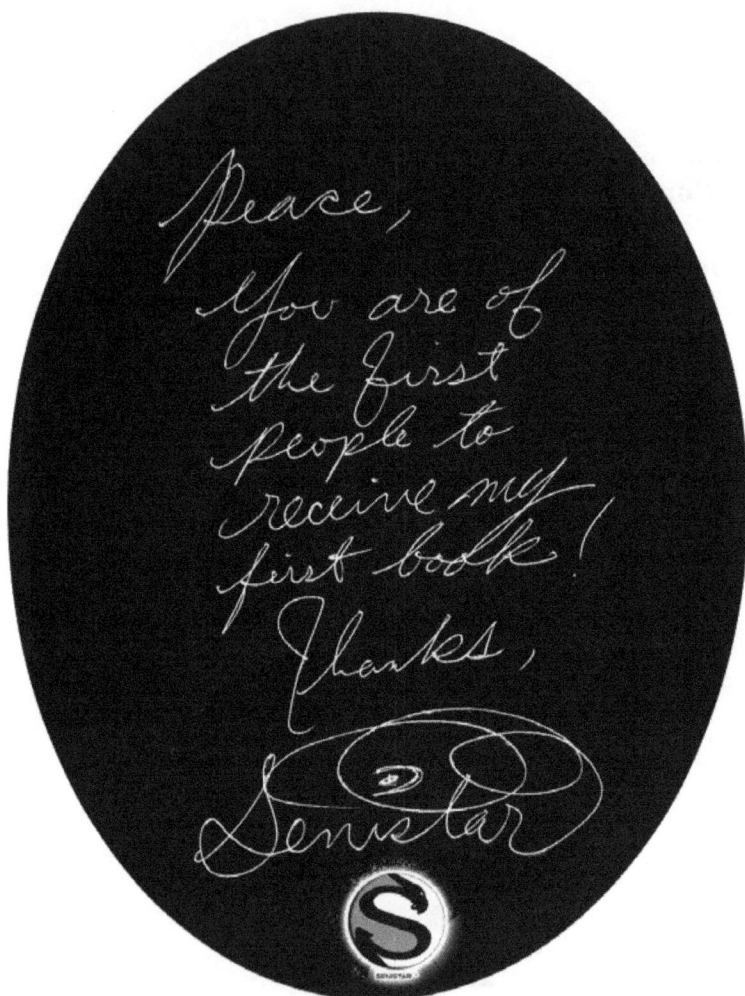

Peace,
You are of
the first
people to
receive my
first book !
Thanks,
Senistar

A courtesy for the 1ˢᵗ 100 owners of "Journeys by Senistar"
We want to hear from you, write:
God's Water Entertainment
Po Box 2085
New York NY 10025
www.Godswater7.com